KEN PIESSE is one of Australia's leading sports writers and his articles on cricket and football appear in newspapers and magazines around the country, including the *Sunday Herald-Sun* in his home town Melbourne. He has written or edited more than a dozen books on cricket and football; the most recent are *Hooked on Cricket* (with Max Walker), the best-selling *Hooked on Football* (with Dermott Brereton) and *Blues, Blinders and Ball-Bursters*.

Ken was a notable suburban footballer himself, playing more than a hundred games with Beaumaris. He is married and has four children.

# PLUGGER
## THE TONY LOCKETT STORY

**TONY LOCKETT**
**WITH KEN PIESSE**

SUN
AUSTRALIA

First published 1992 by Pan Macmillan Publishers Australia
a division of Pan Macmillan Australia Pty Limited
63-71 Balfour Street, Chippendale, Sydney
A.C.N. 001 184 014

National Library of Australia
cataloguing-in-publication data:

Lockett, Tony.
Plugger: the Tony Lockett story.

ISBN 0 7251 0709 X.

1. Lockett, Tony. 2. Australian football—Biography.
3. Football players—Australia—Biography. I. Piesse, Ken. II. Title.

796.336092

Typeset in 10½/11½ Andover by Midland Typesetters,
Maryborough, Victoria.
Printed in Australia by The Book Printer.

# FOREWORD

Anyone in doubt about Tony Lockett's 'Pied Piper' appeal at Moorabbin wasn't at the club's family day on the eve of the 1992 season. I've never seen so many little kids running around with No. 4 on the backs of their St Kilda jumpers.

Tony has a cult following and rightly so. He's the best footballer going around at the present time. Such is his freakish ability and skill, he's capable of becoming one of the all-time champions. He can run, jump and mark brilliantly. He breaks tackles, steamrolls packs and is also a wonderful kick. I don't think he realises how good he really is.

He has always said to me he's going to have a very short career, because of his huge physical build. It would be fantastic if he could play another five or six full years. He could create new goalkicking highs few have even dreamt about.

Injuries have been his problem, yet he's still shown himself capable of coming back midway through a season and kicking the ton.

I've never come across a guy who is so naturally physically strong. We often lined up on each other at match practice and he'd think nothing of giving me a backhander. If he tackled, it was always for keeps.

Like a lot of players from opposition clubs, I always found it better to be behind him than in front of him.

Imagine getting that job as a blocker or having to be the guy to fill up a hole ahead of Tony. You're on a hiding every time the ball comes down.

When he busts through the packs, he really wants to hurt people. There are no beg pardons—whether it be in a practice match or the real thing. It doesn't matter who you are, once he gets on that field, he's fair dinkum. He gives 110 per cent.

We'd have a few drinks after a game and he'd lay these huge bear hugs on me and say: 'I used to love watching you. I want to be like you', and all this sort of stuff. I'd be gasping for breath by the time he let go.

I was lucky enough to play a few years with him and it really meant a lot to me to be highlighted by him in his recent video—also called 'Plugger'.

When we played together I quickly learnt how upset he got if he happened to have a bad day. Many a time I'd see him after the game and know that he just wanted to go home. I'd casually ask him how his dogs were going and that would be it. I knew when to talk to him and when not to talk to him. Unfortunately, other people didn't. They'd stick their noses in and tell him, after he'd kicked eight or nine, that he should have kicked twelve. No wonder he exploded.

In our junior development squads, Tony was always bigger and taller than the others. He played centre half-forward then, and was clearly a League player in the making.

He worked at the King Club with me for a while, as maintenance manager. The ladies used to love him. He was baby-faced and shy and never talked much. They'd bring him in casseroles, soups and sandwiches, home-made pies, the lot. There was enough food for ten men. He'd thank them very much and then neatly stack up what he couldn't eat in his garden shed at home. I went around there one day and found all this food, all untouched and nicely curdled!

Now we do sportsmen's nights together and have developed a funny little routine. I have some set questions I ask him—like is it true that the number of fast food outlets at Cranbourne increased dramatically when they realised you were living in the district and so on. We go through his whole career and all the highlights, which he talks about in this book.

Tony is a very sincere and caring person, who likes his own space. I've always felt if the pressure got too much for him, he might even give footy away. And wouldn't the game be the loser if that ever happened.

He has an awesome on-field presence and I have no doubt that St Kilda is a ten-goal better side when Tony plays. The St Kilda players certainly walk taller when he's around. It's just like in the 1970s when Carl Ditterich was in the St Kilda team. Everyone used to lift. There was an aura around him. It's the same with Tony.

In my last years at St Kilda, I often found myself filling in for him at full forward, especially in 1988–89 when he was out with injury a lot. It was impossible to fill his shoes. I never kicked more than six in a game. If I was lucky it'd be three or four.

Running out side-by-side with him, you just know the team is going to do well. One day at Footscray, Tony ran through Ricky Kennedy and as tough as Ricky was, he was down for keeps. You could sense the Footscray blokes losing confidence after seeing that.

With guys like Tony, Stewart Loewe and Nicky Winmar in the side, St Kilda can win a flag. On their day the Saints are as good as anybody.

It's been an honour to contribute the foreword to Tony's first book. I wish him all the best, in front of goal and as a best-selling author!

TREVOR BARKER
Former St Kilda Captain
APRIL 1992

# CONTENTS

# ACKNOWLEDGEMENTS

I'm very grateful to my good friend and former team-mate Trevor Barker for his kind foreword and also to Ian Stewart—one of my greatest early influences—for his introduction.

Many photographers, from the Melbourne and Ballarat papers, have also been very generous. I particularly thank Tony Greenberg and *Inside Football*, Daryl Timms, Graham 'Toad' Smith and Ken Rainsbury, who supplied many of the shots inside the book.

Col Hutchinson compiled most of the statistics and also the list of everyone I've ever played with at St Kilda.

My manager Robert Hession, family and friends have all been very supportive. Dad goes to every game I play, no matter where it is. Mum has kept scrapbooks since I was knee high.

Ken Piesse's expertise and guidance were invaluable in helping me to prepare the manuscript.

# INTRODUCTION

I'm very proud of what Tony Lockett has achieved and follow his success very closely. From his early teen years, we knew he had unusual ability and I'm sure none of the people involved in his recruiting, Ian Drake, Stuart Trott, Graeme Gellie and myself, are surprised at his progress.

Tony was a shy, big kid when we first talked to him. For me, the impressive part of his game was that he had the skills of a ruck-rover.

He could:
• Kick with both feet;
• Had the unusual ability to recover once the ball hit the ground;
• Possessed explosive pace over five metres;
• Could 'read' where the ball was going;
• Was a most unselfish, team-orientated player;
• And, he had a habit of 'hanging' in the air for his marks, being able to come in from either his left or right side, a skill usually reserved for the best smaller players.

With more stamina, I felt he could have played in almost any position, which again was most unusual for such a big fellow. He also had fire in his belly. Even then, you wouldn't want to have said much wrong to him, on or off the field. He didn't take any nonsense from anybody.

In his first year, as a 17-year-old, he'd played just a few senior games for us before he was selected to represent Victoria in the Teal Cup carnival under the 'King of the Kids', Ray 'Slug' Jordon. We had to talk him into playing, believing it was good for the club's image to see young players playing at such an elite under-age level.

1

He turned out for us in the seniors on the Saturday and flew to Darwin the following day, an all-day trip stopping all stations, and arrived there late on the Sunday night.

He played the following day and Jordon was unhappy with the way he was playing. He thought Tony was a bighead and sent out an uncomplimentary message, via his runner Shane O'Sullivan. Tony promptly told Shane where Jordon should jump off. He was dragged.

When we heard that, we thought, 'That's our Tony'.

'Slug' thought he'd never make it, but Tony had nothing to prove then. He was already playing senior football. He wasn't going to be stood over by anybody.

In some respects he was an angry young man, but any sportsman who has ability invariably has some fire. Tony was shy, but he was also very good. He reminded me of one of the great black sportsmen with some of his mannerisms and skill.

The head of St Kilda's junior development programme, Ian Drake, was the first to spot him. It was my job to contract him and work out what he was worth. Tony was one of six kids we signed on a five-year contract. We gave them each $2000.

Every time Tony played well, he wanted another five-year contract. To my knowledge, he'd had five of them in less than a decade of League football! Under normal circumstances he should have been playing in our under-19s and mixing with kids his own age. He naturally got homesick and even went home a few times, saying he was finished with League football. He was thrust into a situation he shouldn't have been in. Just imagine a kid graduating from the under-16s into League football in just over six months. It was a huge step. But we were last, under extreme financial difficulty and felt our only way out was to go with the kids. We established a junior development programme so we could pinpoint the best youngsters interstate and in our zones, get them into the senior side and leave them there, hoping that they would become ten-year players. Tony was one, David Grant and Micky Dwyer others. Injuries shortened Rod Owen's career, but he had the talent.

We deliberately pushed them, even at the exclusion of established senior players—who at that stage of their careers were a lot better than 16 or 17-year-olds. Among those to leave were our senior and reserves full forwards, Mark Jackson and Mark Scott. We felt Tony needed the experience of playing the position and he needed games under his belt.

We knew he had a wonderful future. Some didn't agree that he should be put into the seniors so quickly, but the decision was made at club level. An opening was made and Tony's career took off.

Several times in his early games, he ended matches close to tears. Mark Jackson would encourage him on the training track but as soon as he started kicking goals, Mark realised he was a danger to his own position and often in Tony's first matches, insisted on him playing a forward pocket role way up the ground, often up near the wing. He told others like Silvio Foschini to do the same thing. That was ridiculous. It really meant that 'Jacko' had to kick fourteen goals himself every week for us to have a sniff of winning.

For a brief period, Tony became inhibited and lost confidence, but after eighteen months, given the no. 1 job at full forward, he felt more at ease with playing League football and was never again intimidated by an opponent or a team-mate.

It's hard to know how far Tony can go with his football. None of us will know until he plays a full season again, like he did in 1987 when he won the Brownlow. Certainly the League's goalkicking record of 150 is in jeopardy.

I rate Tony superior to Peter Hudson and Doug Wade, the greatest full forwards of my era. They played in better teams than him and in Hudson's case, many of his goals came at tiny Glenferrie Oval, where his opportunities were more numerous than on more expansive grounds.

I wouldn't be surprised if Tony kicked 180 goals one season. He's that good.

IAN STEWART
Triple Brownlow Medallist
BRISBANE MAY 1992

How sweet it is! My 100th goal, 1987; the first time I'd achieved three figures in my life.

# 1 ALL YOU WANTED TO KNOW
# ABOUT TONY LOCKETT

FULL NAME:  Anthony Howard Lockett.

BIRTHPLACE:  St John of God, Ballarat.

WEIGHT THEN:  8 lb 4 oz.

AGE:  26.

HEIGHT:  191 cm (6 ft 3 in).

WEIGHT NOW:  It varies!

SCHOOLS:  Forest Street Primary and Wendouree High Technical School.

FOOTBALL CLUBS:  North Ballarat, St Kilda.

OCCUPATION:  Professional footballer.

HOME CITY:  Ballarat.

MARITAL STATUS:  Single.

BOYHOOD HERO:  Leigh Matthews.

PERSONAL HIGHLIGHTS:  Winning the Brownlow, a couple of Coleman Medals and two club best and fairests. The 1991 final series was also great.

WORST INJURY:  Either my knee or ankle have been my worst ones.

MAJOR INTERESTS:  Greyhounds, indoor cricket, water skiing – most sports.

AMBITION:  To be successful; win a Grand Final.

MY BEST YEAR:  1989 was going to be before it was cut short. If I had another year like 1991, I'd be happy.

FAVOURITE GROUNDS:  Moorabbin and the MCG.

MOST ADMIRED PLAYER: Danny Frawley.

PEOPLE I OWE MOST TO IN FOOTBALL: My father, 'Plugger' snr.; Ian Stewart; Ian Drake and Graeme Gellie who all helped in giving me a start; Darrel Baldock.

THE BEST TEAM OF MY TIME: Hawthorn had it over almost everybody in the 1980s and early 1990s. I didn't play in my first winning team against them until 1990 when we won at Moorabbin by three points.

TODAY'S GAME: It's going the right way for the sports-loving spectator. But it's very hard and demanding on the players with the training schedules they now have lined up for us. We're playing games on Friday nights, Saturday, Sunday and some Mondays. It's very tough on a player having to play in Perth on a Sunday and front up for work back home on the Monday.

CAREER EXPECTANCY: Another five years.

## FAVOURITES

FOOD: Roast lamb.

DRINK: Coke.

MAGAZINE: *Greyhound Weekly*, expertly edited by Alan Julien and Peter Quilty.

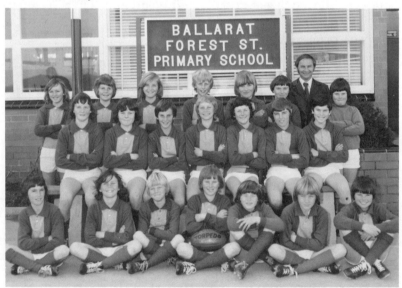

Our old school team, Forest Street Primary, Ballarat. I'm in the front row, second from the right.

6

With 'Doc' Baldock after kicking seven goals in our defeat of Melbourne at Moorabbin, in May 1988.

BOOK: Dermott Brereton's *Hooked on Football*.

MOVIE: *Escape from Alcatraz*.

MUSICIAN: Jimmy Barnes.

HOLIDAY PLACE: Queensland.

SPORTSMAN: Jeff Fenech.

TV SHOW: I don't watch much telly. I used to like Graham Kennedy's *Coast to Coast*. He was good value.

# 2  HOW COULD I
## HAVE MISSED?

## THE ECSTASY AND THE AGONY OF OUR FIRST FINAL, 1991

I don't think I've ever missed four easier shots.

Elimination Final day, 1991, our first appearance in a final in eighteen years, could have been the start of something great. Ultimately it spelled our premature exit from the premiership race.

For days I wondered what could have been. Deep down, I knew I could have kicked those goals in the first quarter. Had I done so, it might have been a different story.

What was really upsetting was that two of the goals were from point-blank range. They should have been sodas. Perhaps my missing the goals had an effect on all the other blokes. After all, kicking goals from 20 and 30 metres out is a full forward's bread and butter. There's no way you should miss from there. Maybe that did take its toll and the others thought: 'Jesus Christ. What's happening?'

Months after the event, I still don't have an explanation. Maybe I was more uptight than I thought. Maybe I was holding back a bit. I know everyone was pretty jumpy, but I felt good. Pre-match I was nice and comfortable and very strong within myself.

It was good to get a couple of grabs early and I didn't panic after those early misses. I said to myself: 'The next one is twice as important now. Get the next one.'

In retrospect, if I had kicked the early goals, we might have settled down and just gone bang, bang, bang. We would have

Taking a snap shot ahead of Andrew Rogers during the 1991 elimination final against Geelong. I got enough of the ball, but not enough of them went through.

been off and away. But that wasn't the way it went. We lost a couple of players early in the game and had no interchange for the rest of the match.

The two guys sidelined, David Grant and Nathan Burke were enormous losses. 'Granty' is like a brick wall in the backline, while if you want someone put off their game, 'Burkey' is the one to do it. Nine times out of ten, he negates his opponents to nothing. With those two going off, we lost a lot of power, a lot of defence, a lot of everything.

At half-time we led by more than three goals, only to see Geelong hit back in the third quarter and take a one point break coming into the last term.

9

Left: Gee, it was disappointing walking off the ground, knowing our run at the premiership was over after just one match. Gilbert McAdam (right) and Dean Greig are pictured with Geelong's Andrew Bews.

Right: Nathan Burke has become one of our key running players, with a knack of restricting big-name opponents.

Halfway through that last quarter I still thought we had them. I felt comfortable and confident that we were just about ready to break their hearts. But it didn't happen and despite us taking that early lead, they ended up beating us. (By seven points, after the lead changed seven times during the match.)

A week later, Geelong was only just rolled by Hawthorn, the eventual premiers.

I still reckon we should have beaten Geelong that beautiful, spring day in September 1991.

People are right when they say finals football is something different. Running out, I saw hundreds of fans with their faces painted red, black and white. The crowd just roared all day.

Gee, it was disappointing walking off the ground, knowing we'd been beaten. As the siren blew, I shook hands with Barry Stoneham, who'd been moved back on to me, and wished him all the best for the remaining couple of games that they were going to play in. I also went over to a young bloke who used to play with us, Sean Simpson. He's a good friend of mine and I repeated what I'd said to Barry.

At the race all the blokes had their heads down. We were

10

pretty devastated. Inside, Kenny Sheldon kept saying to us: 'Just keep your heads up blokes. You did the best you could. That's all we can ask.'

Everyone gave 100 per cent. It was just unfortunate at the end of the day, that the result wasn't in our favour. But that's football. You can sum it up and say: 'Well, at least we got to the finals.' But that's not quite good enough. Our best may have been a little bit better than Geelong's but we took longer to get into the action.

We know we weren't far off in 1991 and after years of being down the bottom, that was really saying something.

Our form had been pretty good all year. We beat Hawthorn at our only meeting and it could be argued that we were just as good a side.

Hawthorn have had enormous finals experience and know how to perform at their best when it counts. With St Kilda, it was the first time most of us had ever played in a final. Maybe that was a factor.

Maybe we did have a few too many nerves, but I felt we played very professionally that day. 'Bomba' Sheldon had all the guys fired up at the right time. Looking back at it now, no-one should blame themselves. I don't think the loss will hurt us at all. Now we have the chance to do better and qualify higher.

We now know what to expect next time we get there. Getting the taste of it was one thing. Now, hopefully, all the blokes are a little hungrier and we'll turn the loss around to work in our favour in the years ahead.

Marking ahead of Geelong's Ken Hinkley for one of my nine goals.

# 3 HEADING FOR
## THE FINALS

Season 1991 was a topsy-turvy year for me. Again I failed to play anything like a full season, this time because of a cracked vertebra in my lower back, after I'd cannoned into Eagle Steve Malaxos in a pre-season game. I trudged from the ground at a snail's pace and went straight up the race. I knew something was badly wrong.

It took me two months to get over that one. It was a very frustrating time, especially as the original diagnosis had been just a badly bruised back.

We played good football as a team though, and for the second time in my career I kicked 100 goals,* which was very satisfying. An even better accomplishment as far as I was concerned was that for the first time in almost twenty years, St Kilda made the finals.

I doubt I would have broken the 150 goal record in 1991, even if I had played a full season. Records don't really mean a great deal to me anyway. I'm just happy to go along, win the games and get into the finals. That is what I want out of football.

I came back after my injury pretty hungry for success. I'd had to sit in the stands while we tied with Collingwood, the defending champions, and then saw us go down to Carlton at Princes Park. Actually I wanted to play that game, but the match committee felt I should have another week off.

* He finished with 127 goals in seventeen games, at an average of 7½ a game. On a record six occasions he kicked ten or more goals in a match, including twelve, ten and twelve in consecutive matches, equalling the feats of Bob Pratt (South Melbourne in 1934) and John Coleman (Essendon, 1953).

12

Coming into our round 10 game with Essendon, I'd kicked 34 goals in my only three games of the 1991 season, but was held to four by Anthony Daniher and co. The Bombers played eight defenders that day.

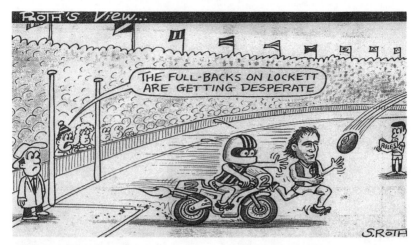

This cartoon took my fancy.

In my first game back, against Adelaide, I kicked twelve for the day, including nine before half-time. I got double figures in the next two games, too, against Brisbane and Sydney, but everything came unstuck against Essendon. We lost at home by almost five goals and I kicked only four. Everyone said how great Anthony Daniher played. He did. But they didn't say anything about the two extra blokes he had helping him who were standing about 20 or 30 metres in front of him all day. It's hard enough to beat one bloke on his merits, let alone two or three. But that's part and parcel of the game. It worked for them that day. They won. That's the way it goes.

We had many team highlights in 1991, but after a good start, we suffered three straight losses late in the season, to fall from third to sixth leading into the important match against Carlton in round 21. We were playing at Waverley, a ground where our record was less than good. We started well and had a great nine-goal win.

It was a memorable day for me. The ground was in excellent condition and I kicked 13.3, lifting my tally to 97 for the year. Five of my goals came in the last quarter as we ran away with the match. It was the most I'd ever kicked in a proper game before.* The whole team played well that day, and it gave us great confidence that we could play well anywhere.

Our match with the Crows, the following Friday night in Adelaide, was also crucial. The Crows had played really well

* He kicked 13.1 against Essendon in a practice match at Cohuna in 1989.

14

Making space and marking ahead of Jon Dorotich during the Carlton game.

at home all year and, before the game, Kenny Sheldon told us just how important it was to start the game well.

Adding to the pressure was the prospect of my one-hundredth goal. Happily, everything worked out, right from the start. I kicked a couple of early ones to reach 99 and a minute into the second quarter I got my one-hundredth, via a daisy-cutting pass from Danny Craven, which I just got to after throwing myself forward like a slips fielder in cricket. There was no crowd stampede this time, which suited me. People mean well, but when you get 400 pats on the same spot on the back, it starts to hurt a bit!

We ran away to win by eight or nine goals and I got 10.6. I missed a few I felt I should have got, but overall I was pretty rapt. We'd put some space between the seventh and eighth sides and were heading for the finals.

That night, Craig Devonport and I went to the Adelaide casino. I was given $1000 worth of chips to play with, but I'm not a big casino man. I wouldn't even know how to play those games.

We pottered around for about an hour and after we'd chucked $50 on the blackjack table and lost that within five minutes, I said to 'Devo': 'It's no good the rest of it going like that. We might as well put it in our pockets and bolt.' And we did, with $950 in the kick.

Left: On the way to thirteen goals against Carlton.

Right: Five goals in the last quarter, thirteen for the game and 97 for the year. Walking into the rooms (past Eddie Melai) after our important win against the Blues. We followed with a big win in Adelaide to consolidate a finals berth.

Apparently a few people were surprised at that, but I'd been there for an hour and I wouldn't even have gone but for the special invitation. The only thing I bet on is the dogs.

# 4 BORN TO PLAY
## FOOTBALL

Howard 'Plugger' Lockett, my Dad, played more than 500 games of football in the Ballarat and Lexton leagues. He was captain-coach of Lexton and captain-coach of North Ballarat reserves before coaching the senior side for quite a few years.*

With Dad so involved in the game, there was never a shortage of footballs around home. I had a football in my hand from the minute I woke up to the minute I went to sleep. I loved it that much. It meant everything to me.

I'd kick the footy before school, after school and all hours into the night. I can't remember how many pairs of shoes I went through. But they always wore out in the same spot, at the end of the right foot.

There was a vacant block over the road from our place where Dad set up some goalposts. Before that, I used to kick on the road, aiming between a telegraph pole and a tree.

Kicking the footy on the road was the done thing then. Everybody did it. You don't see too much of it now, though there's one keen young bloke up the road from me who comes over for a kick after school.

Just like Dad, I was always competing. At the end of a session with him, there'd invariably be one minute to go in the grand final and my side would just happen to be five points down— I liked to make it nice and dramatic. If I happened to miss, it was always because the imaginary bloke on the mark had cribbed and I'd be entitled to another kick.

* Howard Lockett played 150 junior, 60 reserves and 143 senior matches with North Ballarat and 153 with Lexton, where he coached four flags and played in two others. He coached North Ballarat to premierships in 1978 and 1979 as well as coaching the Ballarat interleague side in 1979-80.

17

Left: Training (aged 15) with Dad at North Ballarat.
Right: I had a football in my hand from the minute I woke up to the minute I went to sleep. Me in my North Ballarat jumper, 1977.

When Dad, my brother Neil, or my friends weren't available, I'd kick by myself. It didn't worry me either way, though my Dad still talks about how I drove him around the bend nagging at him to come out. Nothing's changed. I still drive him around the bend.

Dad could kick them all—drop kicks, torpedoes, the whole works. He still says he taught me how to kick. He reckons my initial instinct was to throw the ball around when I was kicking. He insisted on my using both feet, left and right. 'The younger you start, the easier it is,' he'd say.

I'm glad I listened. To this day, Danny Frawley still can't kick on his left foot. If you start when you're young, it seems to come naturally. But if you start when you're 16 or 17, it takes you that much longer to learn.

I went along to the North Ballarat games, but can't remember Dad much as a player. I was the team mascot on a couple of occasions. The rest of the time I busied myself getting into mischief up the back of the grandstand.

I used to suffer from knock knees pretty badly in those days and had to spend nights in bed with calipers on to try and rectify the problem. I'm not sure how long it went on for but it wasn't very enjoyable, I remember that.

18

I was built like a rover then. There was hardly anything of me at all.

For years I pestered Mum and Dad to let me play with the club's under-12 team. Finally they relented. I'd just turned seven.

I didn't get too many kicks in my first year, but I vaguely recall kicking a goal in my first practice match—at training—so I must have been positioned somewhere near the goals, which consisted of two old 44-gallon drums.

We trained twice a week, Mondays and Wednesdays, at the Showgrounds. All the under-14s, under-16s and under-18s trained, too. There were kids everywhere. The coaches used to split the four sides up into sections of the ground. As the littlest kids, we had to use the makeshift goals.

I started off as a rover and a ruck-rover before, as I grew, progressing into a ruckman and centre half-forward. I was always a pretty skinny sort of kid, though reasonably tall, I suppose, for my age group.

All of us, my sisters Diane and Carol, and my brother Neil, are into sport. Neil, 21 in 1992, started playing footy when he was very young but switched to basketball. Diane and Carol play top-grade basketball, Diane with Ballarat Miners and Carol with Kilsyth. They have maintained their interest right through.

Mum and Dad liked us all to play as many sports as we

## The Silver Footballer

### This is to Certify that

Tony Lockett *can*

1. Kick a drop punt, torpedo and drop kick with both feet while running forward.
2. Mark a ball over the head kicked from 10m.
3. Handpass a ball 2m to another player while both running (both hands).
4. Run 50m bouncing a football with alternate hands under 12 secs.

PRESENTED BY THE JUNIOR FOOTBALL COUNCIL OF VICTORIA

11. 5.77

Date

Instructor

A 'Silver Footballer' award, courtesy of the Junior Football Council of Victoria.

19

Winning the under-12 doubles in the Ballarat Churches Tennis Association in 1977, with a friend, Brendan Bawden.

could manage. Mum has always played a lot of sport and Dad comes from a sports family so I guess we were always going to be pretty sports-minded. Mum and Dad ran around madly, driving us to training and various venues.

I tried everything: badminton, tennis, table tennis, basketball, football, cricket, the whole lot.

When I was old enough, Dad used to let me come along and join in with the seniors for a little bit of circle work. Even at that early age, football meant everything to me. I'd train Mondays and Wednesdays with the kids and be back there again on Tuesdays and Thursdays.

It was a big thrill to be involved with the senior blokes. It was a good learning process too.

Football was always my No. 1 aim. It was always what I wanted to do. I used to play in the top-grade juniors at tennis and was handy at most sports I tried,* but football was the one that meant the most to me. Certainly I considered it more important than my schooling.

I never did much homework. I wasn't really good at school. It was hard enough to get me to work at school, let alone bring it home and do it there. I could do the work, but I just wouldn't apply myself.

I lived for recess and dinner time when you could get out and have a kick. My friends and I were just normal sorts of kids. It wouldn't matter to us if it was 30 degrees outside. We'd still have a kick.

I went to school at Forest Street Primary and Wendouree High Technical School before leaving after fourth form and going to the School of Mines in Ballarat to do carpentry. I wasn't very successful there either. I didn't show up often enough.

I don't think Mum and Dad ever expected me to go far at school—to get my Higher School Certificate or to be any sort of Einstein. But if a letter was sent home from school, especially around report time, I used to get a fair roasting.

I was just a normal, young boisterous bloke at school who rebelled against going. My report cards aren't that flash. Mum might have burnt them by now.

* In December 1981, Lockett, then 15, representing Ballarat against East Gippsland in the Victorian country under-16 schoolboy cricket championships at Wangaratta, took 9-65 from 21 overs.

State under-16 cricket champions, 1981. I'm in the middle of the extreme back row.

21

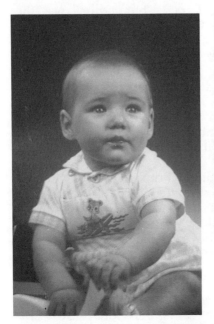
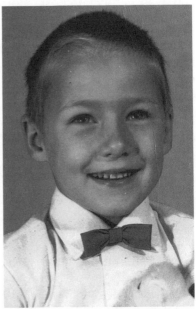

Top left: My earliest baby photo.

Top right: A dapper young man, obviously in tune with fashion, even then . . .

Bottom: The Lockett kids, myself, Neil, Di and Carol.

Top left: With Diane and Dad.
Top right: Plugger snr and jnr—me in my first footy jumper, aged two and a half.
Bottom left: Cheer squad practice for Dad and Lexton.
Bottom right: More happy snaps.

# 5 DEBUTING FOR ST KILDA, AGED 10

As a very young fella, I barracked for Richmond at the prompting of my grandfather, Charlie Lockett. When he died, that was about the end of them for me.

Richmond didn't seem to have too much success, so I got on the Hawthorn bandwagon. I idolised blokes like Leigh Matthews and Peter Knights.

Mum and Dad were mad Collingwood supporters and we used to get down to matches whenever we could. I'd play in the morning for North Ballarat before going down to Melbourne with them for the League game—Collingwood versus whoever.

On two occasions, during my last two years in the under-12s, I came down to represent St Kilda's Little League team. Both matches were at Moorabbin. We lost the first game but won the second. I was pretty proud of that. I was captain.

The games consisted of two six-minute halves and if you got two kicks you were lucky. In those days, the proper goals were used. The ball didn't exactly flash from end to end. Now the kids kick crossways with portable goal posts, which is a much better idea.

While I didn't barrack for the Saints, I knew Ballarat was zoned to St Kilda and if I was going to make it, it was going to be as a St Kilda player. I longed for the opportunity to play League football. Just to be given a chance was good enough for me. It didn't affect me who it was with.

As a kid you always want to play for the club you support but that doesn't work out too often. You have to be pretty lucky if it does.

During those under-age years at North Ballarat, I played in some very successful sides. We made eight grand finals in nine

THE STAMINADE LITTLE LEAGUE

SAINTS

CERTIFICATE

Presented to

T. LOCKETT

as a memento of your playing for the

SAINTS LITTLE LEAGUE

during the 1976 Season

Manager _____          Coach _____

Debuting in the Little League, aged 10.

years. The under-12s played off five years in a row, we might have missed one year in the under-14s—when we got to either the first semi or preliminary final—and there were two more grand finals in the under-16s.

Although I won a couple of best and fairests in the juniors, I didn't do it every year or anything like that. But in one of my under-12 games, against Buninyong, I kicked twelve goals, playing as a ruckman/forward. I was pretty pleased about that.

I made some representative sides, and in mid-1982, while I was playing in the under-16s, I was invited to St Kilda by Graeme Gellie, who was the club's Ballarat-based junior development co-ordinator.

We trained on Sunday mornings, as did the club's metropolitan squad (under Kevin Roberts) and the Frankston squad (Stewie Trott).

Once a year, the three squads would assemble at Moorabbin and play a round-robin competition. After our two games, I was voted best player of the carnival and realised then that maybe there was a chance I was going to play League football. Roddy Owen also played in that carnival, but I can't remember too many others going on to become regular League footballers.

I couldn't get enough football then. I thought nothing of

25

Deputy vice-captain of North Ballarat under-12s, 1977. (I'm in the front row, next to our captain Barry Hills, who is holding the footy.) We made five Grand Finals in a row.

Right: Graduating into the under-14s, 1980.

playing two games in row, either with the under-12s and immediately afterwards with the under-14s or later with the under-16s and then the under-18s. I could do it when I was a kid, but I wouldn't go too well now.

Senior football was so very different, like another world. I stepped up from being one of the biggest players in the junior competition where I could virtually do what I wanted, to playing against men. It was a real experience. It took a while to adjust to it, as I was really only a boy.

The games were played so much harder than the under-16s. But it did me the world of good. It opened my eyes. Senior football was what it was all about. It was competitive and I realised it wasn't going to be easy.

Top: On the way to Anglesea for a training camp with St Kilda's Ballarat-based under-17 development squad. I'm fourth from the left. Later that year, I played in Launceston with the overall squad against a Northern Tasmanian schoolboys team.

Bottom: You can't beat that premiership feeling; a second flag with North Ballarat under-16s, 1982.

April 24, 1982. A goal with my first kick with North Ballarat seniors, against Golden Point, eleven minutes into the game, a month after my sixteenth birthday.

I had half a dozen games* in my first year in the seniors, a couple of those on a Sebastopol bloke named Leigh Mitchell, who was built like a proverbial you-know-what and had quite a reputation as one of the rough and tough blokes of the Ballarat League. He never came the dirty or anything like that on me. He had respect for me I suppose and I respected him.

I had a couple of matches in the seniors, and went back and played in the juniors, before having another four matches at open-age level. If I'd played any more senior games that year, I would have been ruled ineligible for the juniors and as it was near finals time, I went back to the juniors, and was a part of another premiership, my fifth since joining the club.

Later that year, around Christmas time, Tony Jewell, Ian Stewart and Graeme Gellie came up and saw me at home. They said they'd like me to come down and try out. They'd organise a house or board and I'd start in the reserves. My dreams were coming true. League football here I come.

---

* His most successful debut game was against Maddingley-Bacchus Marsh when he kicked six goals in a half before dislocating two fingers and not reappearing after half-time. The previous year, aged 15, he'd kicked six goals for the North Ballarat reserves.

# 6 RELUCTANT
## CITY SLICKER

The prospect of playing footy in the Big Smoke appealed to me—but not the idea of having to live away from Ballarat.

I went home heaps of times, intending never to return. I had to virtually be dragged back to Melbourne. A couple of times I missed training altogether, saying to myself: 'No, I'm not going. I've had enough. I don't enjoy it. I want to stay here and play with my mates.'

A lot of country blokes would know how I felt. They would have gone through the same thing, especially at the same age. It's not so bad when you're a bit older, perhaps 20 or 21. But when I first moved down, I was just 16 and hated it.

It was January 1983 and I moved in with Stewie Trott and his family down at Frankston for the first few weeks. They were very kind, but to me, it was like living in another world. I'd just come from playing under-16s and had all my mates at home. At that time I was really finding out what life was all about. All of a sudden I was shoved down to Melbourne and confronted by all these training schedules. I was so uncomfortable with it that by the time the first game came around, I was living back in Ballarat. I'd lasted only a few months.

It took a good twelve months before I got used to Melbourne to any degree. It was a completely different lifestyle. I was used to paddocks and wide open spaces. People were a lot more relaxed and casual back home.

Frankly, I found it pretty overwhelming. Everything was new, the people, the training, the life.

But there was also a certain excitement, especially the idea of playing alongside blokes who had been champion players for years like Trevor Barker. I'd only seen these blokes on television or read about them in the papers. All of a sudden, there I was, rubbing shoulders with them.

I got along all right with all of them—there were no worries from that angle. It just took them a while to accept me and me to accept them. It's the same with any bloke coming into a new club. It takes that little while to get to know everyone and to know what they're like.

Until I got my head known around the joint a bit, the blokes didn't know what I was about and how fair dinkum I was.

I didn't take long to catch on to them all. I was rapt to be training with the seniors. After tasting open-age competition back home, I was glad I didn't have to play in the under-19s.

Mum used to bring me down each Monday. I'd stay Monday night at Greg Packham's flat, train Monday and Tuesday nights, go home with the Ballarat blokes and then come down with them again on Thursday. Three or four of us would pack into three cars and away we'd go. On Saturdays, Mum would bring me down for the games.

That first year was one big learning experience for me. Tony Jewell was a very hard coach, but he was also terrific. He had the loudest voice that I have ever heard. Could he go off! It was unbelievable.

I don't think I ever really got a bad roasting from him. But a couple did. Several times he sent blokes off the training track, after they'd repeatedly made mistakes. If training wasn't what he wanted, he'd get in one of those moods and off they'd go.

I soon noticed the increased training tempo, the intensity and the superior skill levels. Training was a lot quicker and faster, and 'TJ' and the other coaches demanded a lot more effort.

When you kicked to a bloke, you had to hit him. Back home, training was a little bit more lackadaisical. If you made a mistake, it didn't really matter.

I soon became good mates with another young bloke, Rod Owen. Being the same age, 'Rocket' and I used to spend a lot of time together.

Roddy would have to be one of the most gifted footballers I've ever seen. In a practice match against Collingwood in the bush that first year, he kicked seven goals in the seniors, against someone like Billy Picken. He'd only just turned sixteen. I was in the reserves that day and remember sitting on the bonnet of a car watching him play. He was sensational.

Rocket went a bit wayward but he's a terrific fellow. They'll have to make a statue of him when he goes.

Guys like Jeff Sarau and 'Barks' were most helpful to us and all the other young blokes. Both were fantastic clubmen. 'Pup' Sarau was always offering advice.

A couple of times early that season, I played in a forward pocket next to Sarau and he didn't stop talking to me, always being very encouraging. He was really good to play with. Barks was the same, being terrific around the club and mixing in well with everyone. Like Pup, he always had a lot of time for the young blokes. When I first came down, Barks introduced himself and made me feel as comfortable as possible. I've never forgotten that.

# 7 JACKO, SLUG JORDON AND MY DEBUT YEAR

Arden Street, North Melbourne, is not even used for big games any more, but for me it'll always be a special place as that's where I played my very first game, for St Kilda reserves against North Melbourne in the opening round of 1983.

I was picked at centre half-forward but didn't do terribly much early before being moved to full forward where I was opposed by Tim Harrington in the second half. We won and I kicked a few goals (seven)—most of them in the second half. Roy Ramsey was in the opposition but I don't remember too much more about the game. It was a big enough thrill just being out there.

After three games in the reserves I was promoted. I'd kicked just one goal the week before against Hawthorn, but when the teams for the Geelong game at Waverley were read out after training on the Thursday night, I was in the seniors, in a forward pocket next to Mark Jackson.

I started off on the bench and, coming on in the third quarter, managed two goals—including one with my first kick—but we were narrowly beaten. I'm the only bloke from that team still playing there now.

I lasted only one more week before being dropped. We played the Swans in Sydney. 'Jacko' kicked ten and I got only one. It was back to the reserves for me. Later, I was returned to the side, Jacko having left in mid-season.

I've got a bit of time for Jacko, even if he did like me to play forward pocket from the wing. He was one who got out to train early and kicked the footy around a lot.

That first year was a real learning experience for me. Not

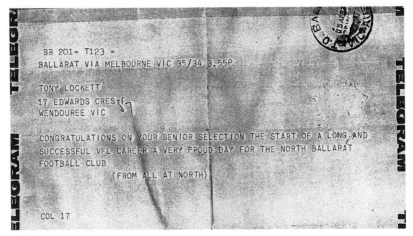

I got a stack of telegrams before my first game, including one from my mates at North Ballarat.

only did I play in the forward line, but I had a taste of defence for the first time. We were playing Carlton at Princes Park and before the match, Tony Jewell came up to me and said: 'I hope you weren't planning on kicking eight today.'

'What do you mean?'

'You're playing full back.'

That was an experience. I lined up on Peter Bosustow, who at every opportunity tried to use my back as a step-ladder. He was very hard to handle. Thankfully they shifted him from full forward to the forward pocket half-way through the first quarter. I didn't worry about following him. I was happy in the goal square—even if it was at the wrong end.

That year, I also represented Victoria in the Teal Cup under-17 competition in Darwin. I'd played on the Saturday against North Melbourne before flying all day on the Sunday and arriving in Darwin late that night for Monday's game.

The heat and the humidity was a killer. I was playing centre half-forward and had kicked four goals up until half-time. I was starting to struggle and a message came out from coach Ray 'Slug' Jordon.

When our full back kicked out, after a behind, I was to lead from centre half-forward, mark it, get back fast and if I could, mark my own kick! It all got a little too much for me. I thought to myself: 'What does this bloke expect of me?'

Whether I got the message mixed up or the runner got the message mixed up, I'm not sure. I sent a message back with him, telling Jordon where to jump off. Actually it was a bit stronger than that. I don't think a kid had ever said that to

Jordon before. But I wasn't going to put up with any rubbish. I was told to come off, which I did. I sat in the dugout, out of the heat, for the rest of the game. And those were virtually the last words Jordon has ever spoken to me. The same goes with Shane O'Sullivan who was the runner!

---

'LIKE A GOD OUT OF GREEK MYTHOLOGY, TONY LOCKETT STOOD STRONG AND TALL AND REFUSED TO GIVE IN TO EVEN THE MOST OVERWHELMING ODDS.'

MALCOLM CONN, AFTER LOCKETT'S SEVEN-GOAL CONTRIBUTION AGAINST GEELONG

(*THE AGE*, 1984)

---

# MY MAJOR
## INFLUENCES

8

Ian Stewart helped launch my career. He got blokes like Roddy Owen and me to St Kilda and was the main man in going for youth at the footy club. He gave us all a chance and an opportunity, seeing that was where the club's future lay. The club didn't have the money to buy big top-name players, and concentrated instead on encouraging young players in its zones.

I can still see Stewie now, on the track, teaching us things and encouraging us all the way. He's one of the men I admire most in football.

I'd love to have seen him play. Apparently he was just a spot-on player. Three Brownlows is a fair effort.

You could tell he could play, even when he was mucking around with us on the track before training. He could drop kick the ball beautifully and had great balance.

All my coaches, naturally, have also had an influence on the way I play today. Tony Jewell* was very straight-forward and very strong-minded. He demanded perfection. And could he yell! All you wanted to do when he yelled was get behind a rock. I reckon he could yell a house down. He wouldn't put up with bad training or anything like that. He demanded that the skill level be high and everyone had to train accordingly. He was a very good coach. He knew what was going on, but probably says now that the administration interfered with him too much.

* Tony Jewell coached St Kilda in 1983–84, being sacked with four games to go in his second season. Graeme Gellie acted as a caretaker coach for the rest of the season before continuing as senior coach in 1985–86. Darrel Baldock coached from 1987–89 and Ken Sheldon from 1990.

'Doc' Baldock's knowledge of the game was virtually unsurpassed.

Graeme Gellie got thrown to the wolves a bit, being rushed into it when Darrel Baldock said no after initially agreeing to coach us. Graeme went from coaching juniors to coaching a League side. He had a lot of very good ideas but didn't quite get the support he should have. When he was there, he gave 200 per cent in everything he did.

'Doc' Baldock's knowledge of the game was virtually unsurpassed. He knew everything, every possible facet, more than anyone that I've ever talked to. Doc knew how to play the game, what to do and when to do it.

He always helped me out, looking after me personally. I'm not saying he gave me special treatment, but whenever I needed something he always helped me. Doc is a real man's man. If you did the right thing by him, he always looked after you.

37

He was a real sticker. I had a lot of time for Doc. Like me, he didn't like training under lights. That suited me down to the ground.

Ken Sheldon lifted us into the finals for the first time in almost twenty years. In less than three full years, he's created a whole new and disciplined attitude at the club. He's the best coach I've ever had. You know if you step out of line one little bit, bang, you'll be fined. It certainly makes you think.

Kenny creates a lot of exuberance and good feeling around the place. Being very well liked, he did that when he was a player, too. That feeling for him has continued in his time as a coach. He may now have a stronger outlook, which is necessary once you coach, but he hasn't lost any of his bubbly personality.

I must have had more fines than anyone in these last two seasons. I copped a $1000 fine for being late to the plane before an interstate trip. Another time I was three minutes late to training one Saturday morning and copped an on-the-spot $1000 fine.

Mind you, training had been called at 6 a.m., so I thought 6.03 a.m. wasn't such a bad effort! It was my own fault, of course. I knew the fuel gauge on my car was low, but instead of stopping and getting fuel on the Friday night, I stopped Saturday morning on the way. If I hadn't stopped, I would have made it on time— but then again I might have run out of petrol.

There's no mucking around with the fines. They're automatically deducted from your match payments. And there's little chance of a successful appeal. Once the match committee decides, that's it.

---

'TONY LOCKETT IS A CHAMPION AND THE BEST FULL FORWARD SINCE DOUG WADE, WHO WAS ALWAYS MY FAVOURITE.'

ESSENDON COACH KEVIN SHEEDY, AFTER LOCKETT HAD KICKED NINE GOALS AGAINST THE

BOMBERS, 1987

---

38

# THE ICING
## ON THE CAKE

9

I was sitting next to Jeff Sarau on the plane back from Sydney, having played my second game in 1983. We were chatting about footy in general and he said to me: 'Listen, if you can kick one goal a quarter, you're doing your job boy.' And that's all I've ever gone by—one goal a quarter and four a match. I know if I play for the whole year and keep to that average, I'm going to score 88. Not too many blokes kick more than that each season.

The bottom line, of course, is winning. It doesn't matter if you kick five, ten or fifteen goals. If you don't win, your effort that day is wasted. While four is my starting point, I do like to get five. Five sounds a helluva lot better than four. If I get four, I'm happy. If I get five I'm really happy. Anything over that is icing on the cake.

I suppose I've always been pretty good at kicking for goal, even as a kid. There haven't been too many games where I kicked more points than goals, so I guess my strike rate is probably more than 50 per cent, which is not too bad. If I can get eight shots at goal, I want to kick a minimum of six. I'd be dirty if I kicked 5.3 and shattered if I kicked 4.4.

In 1992, I kicked 3.6 against Melbourne. You can imagine my fury! Lucky the dogs were running that night. It took my mind off things.

# 10 MAGIC
## MOMENTS

Kicking 100 goals in a season is every full forward's ambition. Some may trot out the line: 'It doesn't matter who kicks 'em, as long as they are kicked,' but they are only half-serious, especially if they happen to be in the 'nervous 90s'.

I've kicked 100 goals twice and it's quite a feeling. The first time, in particular, was special, as only one St Kilda player had done it before.*

The hundred goals was also very important to the team. We were on a roll, having won four matches on end to lift ourselves out of wooden spoon contention. Footscray was headed for the finals, being a game clear in fifth place.

We owed them one. At our previous meeting at Waverley they'd kicked double our score and I'd failed to bother the scorers—for the only time all season. You can imagine how keen we all were.

It was raining when I woke up that morning, but it cleared as I drove down from the hills.

I had 93 goals for the season, and before the game I thought how much I'd like to get the 100 that day. But I realised I had plenty of time and shouldn't be too disappointed if I missed.

I felt good, the team was playing well and by three-quarter time, I had 99, having kicked two in each quarter.

The game was a thriller and I knew any opportunity which came my way had to be converted. Early in the quarter, Roddy Owen set me up with a precision pass but I was so nervous that it hit me on the chest and bounced away. I was wild about

* Bill Mohr kicked 101 in 1936.

40

that one and come the 15-minute mark, even angrier as I still hadn't had a kick for the term and Footscray was within a kick of getting in front.

I was giving myself a nice old talking to, repeating to myself: 'The next time it comes down, you've just got to get it!' Soon afterwards I did get it, via a pass from Alex Marcou, and, trying to stay as calm as possible, punted it through from about 40 metres.

Not only was it my one-hundredth, but it gave us an 11-point break. There were almost 25,000 at Moorabbin that day and I reckon 20,000 of them jumped the fence to try and pat me on the back.

It was like a stampede. I saw them coming, but there was nowhere for me to go. The boys surrounded me as best they could for a bit of extra protection. Trevor Barker was one of the first there and he and Nicky Winmar and Roddy were among those trying to hold people off. Danny Frawley sprinted from the other end of the ground and gave me a bear hug. There were people everywhere. I even saw Molly Meldrum's bald head among the throng. It was amazing.

41

Rick Kennedy, my opponent, added his congratulations. I appreciated that. He's as tough as they come, but he's a good sport.

I reckon the last quarter must have gone close to forty minutes, as it took police at least five minutes to clear everyone off.

If the delay unsettled the Footscray blokes, they certainly didn't show it. Footscray kicked the next two goals and suddenly we trailed. Just as my dream day looked like turning into a team nightmare, Nicky Winmar gained possession and I took off. He's so deadly with his delivery that he can pinpoint where I'm going to be from 40–50 metres. This one never looked like missing me. I marked it and put it through, my eighth for the day and 101st for the season. This time Footscray didn't come back. We were home, by three points. I thought I was rapt until I saw my Dad. In his excitement, he just about ripped my head off in the rooms.

Allan Davis coached us that day, 'Doc' Baldock being in hospital having suffered a mild stroke. Danny and I visited him afterwards before going on to David Grant's 21st birthday party.

It was quite a celebration, but it didn't take me long to get back to reality. By 11 o'clock the next morning, I was back at Miner's Rest putting farm fences up.

That one-hundredth goal created good business for Telecom. I lost count of the telegrams I received. Mum has them all pasted into a scrapbook, along with the congratulations cards and other letters. I particularly appreciated a note from Mavis Mohr, the widow of the late Bill Mohr, the first St Kilda player to achieve the ton. She wrote: 'Please accept my congratulations on equalling the goalkicking record of my late husband, Billy Mohr. Bill would have been the first to congratulate you and I wish you good luck, good fortune and good health in your future with the Saints'.

Dozens of others also sent cards and telegrams. Doug Wade, the great Geelong and North Melbourne goalkicker, sent a note. So did Ron Todd, the legendary Collingwood high flier, and Neil 'Nipper' Tresize, the Minister for Sport and Recreation.

# 11 HOW THE DOC FIRED ME UP
## FOR THE BROWNLOW

I don't think I'd ever seen Darrel Baldock so upset. We'd been walloped by Geelong* and after doing all right for much of that '87 season, I put in a bad one, kicking just one goal.

The Doc was furious and after giving us a nice old serve, told us to be at Moorabbin at 7 a.m. the next day. No-one dared say a word as we trooped in, thankfully all by the deadline. There were no hellos. Doc just started on us, carrying on where he'd left off at Kardinia Park the night before. Then he began going through us, one by one, firing a comment at each player. None of it was complimentary, I can assure you.

It was pretty nerve-racking, sitting in line, waiting to get roared at. I was about the third last. Looking me squarely in the eye, he paused and said: 'And you . . . you've just kicked your hundred goals straight out the door you have.' And he started on the next bloke.

That set me right off. I kept it all in, mind you, but I said to myself: 'Right, I'm going to show you.' A few others must have made similar resolutions because that's when our whole season swung around.

For the first time I could remember, we won five games straight to kiss that dreaded bottom spot goodbye. I started to play consistently, getting something like 50-odd goals in the final eight games and more than a hundred for the year.

Doc was very complimentary on best and fairest night, saying how I'd converted all the shots and done very well. But he'd given me great ammunition on that cold Sunday morning and for that, I'll probably always be grateful!

* 13.20 (98) to 3.9. (27), Lockett's season tally being 63 goals after fourteen matches.

One hundred goals and Victorian selection, 1987.

Marking ahead of Fitzroy's Gary Pert. We won five games on end, a 'first' in my time at the club.

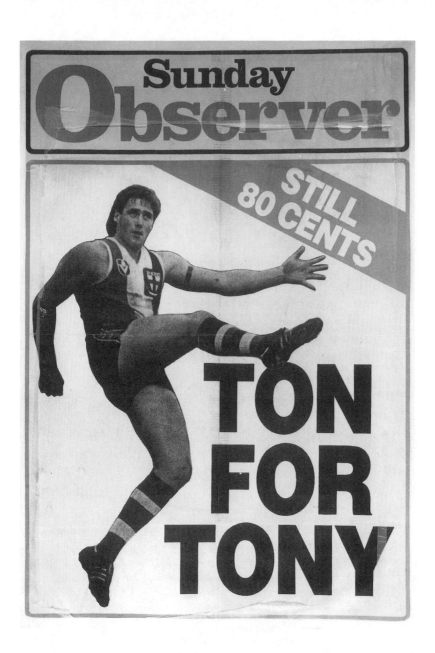

My one-hundredth goal made the newspaper billboards.

# 12 THE NIGHT
## OF NIGHTS

That year I was always one of the so-called Brownlow Medal 'fancies', but as a full forward had never won it before, my expectations were exactly nil. Peter Hudson had kicked 150 one year and been beaten, so how would I go with 117?

Hawthorn's John Platten and other on-ballers had all figured prominently in the other big awards. I thought one of them would win it.

As we finished the season so well and I began to kick big tallies consistently, my priorities firmly centred around winning the club best-and-fairest. If I went well in the Brownlow, I looked upon it as a bonus. Up until round 14 or 15, I hadn't done too much and despite the increasing speculation, felt I'd given away too big a start.

On Brownlow night, I said to Nicky Winmar: 'I've got no hope. We might as well have a night on the League here, mate. Let's hop into the grog a bit,' which we did.

All of a sudden, I went bang, bang, bang. Nine votes in quick time and I was right up there with the leaders. Suddenly I didn't feel like having a drink. It was twenty votes all, Platten and I. I had my head in my hands as the last round of votes was counted. I'll never forget it. I was shaking, and grabbed my girlfriend's hand for comfort.

In the final round, I'd kicked five goals against the Eagles in Perth. But we'd been slaughtered and I didn't think I'd score a vote.

Hawthorn had played Geelong at Kardinia Park. Dad had been down to see it and said Platten had twenty kicks, which was slightly under his average.

C'mon on . . .

C'mon on . . .

Yeesssss!

Vicki and I were embracing. I couldn't believe I'd won it.

The tension was a cracker. It seemed every eye was on me. I was surrounded by newspaper photographers. All the boys were keenly listening, hoping Platten wouldn't break the deadlock.

He didn't get the three. He didn't get the two and he missed a one. There was a roar from the St Kilda tables. I couldn't be beaten.

As the votes for the last games were read out,* Vicki and I were embracing. I couldn't believe it. I was bombarded by people as rapt as me, Danny Frawley, Nicky, dozens of people.

I think I floated to the stage and can't remember too much of my acceptance speech. I was very honoured to be the first full forward to win it, especially considering the champions who'd never won it previously.

Neither Platten nor I had scored a vote in the last round. But I reckon I aged five years in the process. I would have hated to come so close and be beaten by a vote. It would have been heartbreaking. No-one remembers the people who come second.

* As expected, Tony didn't get a vote against the Eagles, and the medal was tied twenty votes all. Both players received a medal, the countback system, where only one winner could be declared, having been abolished in 1981. Under the old system, Lockett would have won, having been voted best afield four times, compared with Platten's three.

Top: I was rapt to have drawn for the Medal. Now I've got my Medal and so has Platten.

Bottom: The Old Cattle Yards Inn was rocking. Dad made sure of that.

I was rapt to have drawn for the medal. Now I've got my medal—or more precisely Mum has—and Platten's got his, too. Good on him I reckon.

It was a huge night. After the interviews and pictures, Vicki and I, Danny and Anita went back to the club, which was packed. I made a phonecall home and everyone was lining up to talk to me, even our bull terrier, Major, who said 'woof' a couple of times.

'Is that you, Major?' I said, and he went 'Woof' again.

Danny and I had booked a room at the Menzies at Rialto, so we went back into town, walked in and a huge party was going on. There were dozens of people there, all whooping it up. Club president Travis Payze and members of the board had ordered big platters of seafood, boxes of Crown Lager and all these expensive wines. It was some party.

I don't think I got to bed until well after five. It was probably closer to six. I slept with the medal around my neck and have the photos to prove it. Apparently, the photographers came in about 6.30 a.m. and found me flaked on the ground, snoring like a baby. I was a terrible looking drunk.

Later that morning I got up, saw the wreckage and realised where I was and what had happened. Going down into the lobby, I thought of the bill. 'This is not going to be real good to hear,' I said to myself. 'But it's going to be worth it anyway. It's only once in a lifetime.'

All the girls were rapt too.

Top: The photographers came in about 6.30 a.m. and found me flaked on the ground, snoring like a baby.

Bottom: My brother, Neil, shares in the fun.

We made the front page of *The Sun*.

Approaching the desk, I said: 'Can I have the bill for room 420?' I got it, blinked at it once and 'Payzey' suddenly appeared from nowhere, and snatched it out of my hand, saying: 'The club will fix this up.'

I was quite happy about that I can tell you. It was for something like $1500! But I still wouldn't have minded because it was a great night, one I'll never forget.

That year had been my best. For the first time I'd played every game, kicked 117 goals and won the Coleman Medal. They gave me 'Goal of the Year' for a boomerang against Footscray and I won the Players' Association's Most Valuable Player award.

I also won *The Age* and *Sunday Press* awards, so I was pretty pleased. Platten had also had a great year and I was thrilled to share the medal with him.

Funnily enough, I missed the award I'd followed closest throughout the year, the one in the *Sun News-Pictorial*. There was good money on offer too, $20,000. Platten and I were neck-and-neck in that one too and it even got to a stage where on Mondays, I'd race down to the shop to see how the votes went. Every time I got three, so did he. He beat me for the twenty grand by a vote or two, but runner-up received $9000 so I didn't complain too much.

I was also presented with the Coleman Medal, named after one of the game's goalkicking greats.

# 13 WHY I THREW
## THOSE CRUTCHES

People say I'm shy, but I'm not. People at St Kilda know that.*
I didn't enjoy being in the limelight much once, but now I'm
a lot more relaxed in my dealings with people. My life is happier
in all respects and it's been good for my footy.

Reporters may say I'm still a bit wary, but I just don't see
the sense of giving interviews and having my face and name
plastered all over the papers every second week. You can create
undue pressure for yourself and trigger higher expectations than
are truly fair.

I'm sure a guy like Dermott Brereton finds it hard to come
up week after week and play to a certain standard, especially
with the injuries he's had. I know I do. No matter who you
are, you're going to have your good days and your bad days.
I suppose no-one wants to know about bad days. If I play a
bad game, the media wants to know why. All of a sudden, I'm
overweight and have been up to this and that.

I know people expect a lot of me, but all the extra headlines
are something I don't want hanging over my head. When you're
playing well, everything is fine and nothing is ever said. They
write you up to be this-and-that, yet the following week they
'can' you. That's hard to take and, in a way, has turned me
off the media a lot.

I don't like to be embarrassed in front of anyone. That's just
the way I am. For a while there, I found it easier just to say
nothing and then no-one had anything on me. For twelve months,

* In 1985 as a fundraiser for the players' trip away, Lockett allowed his tracksuit,
guernsey, shorts and socks to be sold at a club function for $2000. He ended up
stripped down to his Speedos.

Me and my crutches . . . I can look back on it now and laugh.

# Lockett, TV men clash

## Lockett lets fly

### Lockett throws crutch at television crews

### -'Strained' Lockett attacks cameraman

The newspapers had a holiday . . . at my expense.

I don't think I gave an interview. I remained in the background and that is the way I like it.

Sometimes you just want to be left alone. In 1988, five days after breaking my ankle, I went to a hospital about 9 a.m. and out of the blue came a couple of teams of cameras. I think it was Channel Seven and Eddie McGuire and his boys from Channel 10.

I look back on it now and laugh, but at the time I was furious. How did they know my appointment time? No-one was supposed to know except the club and me.

I was limping in on crutches through a side door and here they were filming my every step. What really set me off was that I fell on the mat going inside, went straight over on my backside. I was pretty embarrassed about it. I did my cruet, blaming the camera crew and let them have it, even though it wasn't really their fault.

Aiming the crutches like spears, I pinged them at them, one at a time. I was furious. I didn't do any damage. Neither found their mark, but I got my point across.

If it happened to me now, I'd handle it a bit differently— probably count to ten and then throw them.

57

Seriously though, the media boys have got a job to do and I'm trying to work in with them more. Like anyone, I'd obviously rather read something nice written about me, than something bad. But if I don't feel it's the right time and place to do an interview, I try to be polite about it and say: 'Look if you don't mind I'd rather not say anything. Maybe next time.' Most will accept that. However, you do get some persistent ones.

In 1989, I was fined $1500 for missing State training and for a time there was a risk of me being suspended from a club game. That would have been serious. Channel Seven sent Michael Roberts and a camera crew up to Ballarat to see me. I know Mick and played footy with him, but I was in no mood to talk to anybody.

I was out in my back shed when I saw this car driving up and down the road a few times. Next minute it came straight up the driveway and out the back to where I was.

Mick hopped out, followed by all the camera boys. I saw red: 'Robbo you know what my temper is like mate,' I told him. 'I'd advise you to get back in the car and head off home.' He didn't say a thing, other than 'no worries'.

And at that he turned around, got in the car and they left. Later I felt a tinge of sympathy for Mick—driving all the way to Ballarat and then hardly getting in a word.

I don't think anyone's got the right to invade your home. Everyone is entitled to a certain amount of privacy. If you can't get away from people in your own home, where can you get away from them? I didn't appreciate the way it was handled. It might have been different if Robbo had got the driver to stop out the front, instead of just driving around the back of the house, where I was.

On other occasions, I've had cameramen parked out the front of my house for hours, just sitting there with their cameras ready to roll on anyone coming in or going out. They were like bloody vultures. If that's not intrusive, what is? I don't think anyone should be subject to that. The only way they moved was after I called the police.

# 14  A PAIN IN THE GROIN AND OTHER ASSORTED INJURIES

I have a painkilling injection in my groin every week before I run out. But it's no big deal. It's just become part of the game for me. You'd be surprised how many players have these sorts of injections before the game.

I've lived with a groin problem for a long time now. It's something that I guess is going to be with me for the rest of my football. It's a wear-and-tear injury, from the years of carrying the weight and the work that has been required of me.

The only way to fix a groin is through rest. I have had plenty of that, but it's still not right. If it doesn't get any worse, I will have no problems at all. Once I get out on to the ground, I'm pretty right.

What I do have to be careful about is keeping my weight down, to around 103–105 kg which I regard as ideal.

At times, my weight has ballooned, as high as 113 kg, but I've really struggled at that weight. I was lethargic and felt uncomfortable. It's hard knowing what to do and wanting to do it but not having the physical capacity to do it. I lacked a yard, couldn't jump for marks and ran out of gas.*

Being such a big bloke, I'm pretty hard to shift off the ball. But if I get too heavy, my mobility suffers and opposing players can run off me too easily.

* Lockett's huge frame is a common discussion point. During the 1986 pre-season, Lou Richards, writing in *The Sun*, commented: 'For the past three years, Tony Lockett has been St Kilda's answer to American football star William "the Refrigerator" Perry. Since he joined the club in 1983, the Saint full forward has carried more blubber than a Japanese whaler. The joke at Moorabbin was that the Saints warmed up by doing two laps around Lockett'.

Injured against the Eagles in the Foster's Cup, 1991. Initially I was told it was only a bruised back, but it just wouldn't come good. Talk about a frustration. I had to sit out the first third of the 1991 season.

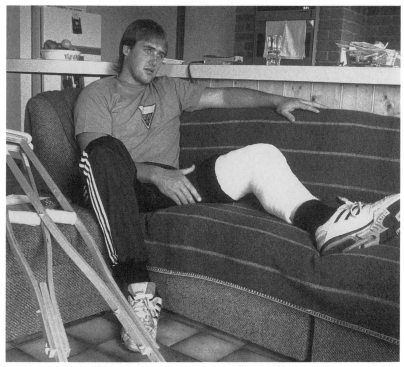

I did my knee against North Melbourne. I knew it was serious as soon as I'd done it.

Over the years, there have been many, on and off the field, who have had a go at me about my weight. Sure I've missed more games than most, but I don't think my weight was responsible for my injuries, other than my groin.

People mightn't agree but you're never going to be able to change what people think. Take my ankle injury against Footscray\*, for example. It was a freak accident, a case of being in the wrong spot at the wrong time. I led for a ball from Stewie Loewe, went up and came down right on the ankle. There was nothing I could have done about that.

My knee was just the same. It was just a freak accident, and with my back last year, there was nothing I could have done about that one. I just copped a knee in the wrong spot, in a collision with Steve Malaxos. So I don't really see how my weight can be blamed.

Injuries are part and parcel of a game of football. Sometimes you're still able to hobble around and contribute. At other times, you have no choice but to come off.

\* In the 11th round of the 1988 season.

Injured against Footscray. There was nothing I could have done about it.

I did my knee against North Melbourne, close to the half-way mark of the 1990 season. I knew it was serious as soon as it happened. I tried to get through a pack and got a knock on it.

But I had to keep my place in the team on the ground that day. Earlier in that match, I sensed it was a turning point for me. I was just starting to find a bit of form. I was running and hitting the ball pretty hard before it happened. I felt good, having kicked a few goals (five) up until half-time, including four in the first quarter.

Just after I hurt myself, North moved John Longmire up on to me. He'd beaten me the year before in a night game at the MCG and I thought to myself: 'I remember this bastard. I want to fix this bloke up.'

As it turned out, I got only another kick or two, but my knee was crook. It was very frustrating. I had so much bloody tape wrapped around my knee that I could hardly move. Longmire was running off me to the point where it was becoming embarrassing. It hurt my feelings a bit. As I went off, I told him I'd even the score. Most footballers have long memories. I know I do.

# 15 MARKED
# MEN

Players like Dermott Brereton and myself get more attention than other blokes. That's a fact of life.

Sometimes he hasn't been in the mood to handle it. Neither have I.

It's all right to be in control of the situation but, like Dermott, I've always believed you have to stand up for yourself. You can't just let yourself be manhandled by your opponent all day. You're not going to be any good for anyone—yourself, your club or your team-mates—if you allow a bloke to hang on to you all day and impair your leads. You've got to do something about it.

A few years ago, I couldn't hold my temper. When she blew, she blew. If I was going to go for one punch I'd go for ten.

In round one, 1988, at the Western Oval, Rick Kennedy kept holding on to my jumper. Try as I might, I couldn't get away from him. In the third quarter, I went to make a lead, but again was impeded. I thought to myself: 'This has got to stop.' I turned around and that was it, we were into it. I threw punches like bloody windmills. We both landed on the ground, me on top. All I wanted to do was keep throwing them.

It felt good at the time. I let off a lot of steam but after it got broken up, four umpires got me for striking. Almost immediately, I thought to myself: 'Well a bloke is a bloody idiot for doing that. Now I'm going to sit out for a month.' (I was suspended for two weeks.)

I guess I was just young and stupid. Five minutes later, I chased Kennedy out of the forward line, doing my best to keep the pressure on him.

Top: Dermott Brereton and I attract more than our fair share of the headlines. Sometimes he hasn't been in the mood to handle it. Neither have I.

Bottom: Going over the top against Collingwood's Jamie Turner. It was only a slight miscalculation. I was going for the ball, but Stewie Loewe got there first!

Top: I turned around and that was it, we were into it.
Bottom: I threw punches like bloody windmills.

66

Almost immediately, I thought to myself: 'A bloke is a bloody idiot for doing that. Now I'm going to sit out for a month.' John Russo was one of three umpires to book me.

He was calling for a handball and wasn't looking where he was running. From over his shoulder, I could see my team-mate Greg Burns coming at him at 100 miles an hour. I thought to myself: 'This poor bloke. He's going to get it'.

And he did. 'Burnsey' hit him right up the middle and Kennedy went down like a sack of spuds. I thought there was no way known he could have got up, but to the bloke's credit he did.

There wouldn't be too many blokes who could have done that after Burnsey had dealt with them. I figured Kennedy earned his stripes that day. He was tough all right. And he's got a bloody hard head.

I also lost my temper with Laurie Serafini of Fitzroy one day. He held on to my jumper once too often. It's one thing I don't take too kindly to. I lost control for half a minute and ended up getting pinged by three umpires. (I got a week.)

One thing, though. Not too many hold my jumper now.

———•———

'SAINTS SPEARHEAD TONY LOCKETT AND SOARING HAWK DERMOTT BRERETON HAVE AN EXTRA HANDICAP THIS SEASON—SHARP KNIVES. THE KNIVES ARE NOT WIELDED BY SURGEONS BUT CRITICS WHO DELIGHT IN CHOPPING TALL POPPIES. BUT BOTH TONY AND DERMOTT ARE PROFESSIONALS WHO DEAL WITH THEIR DETRACTORS THE BEST WAY POSSIBLE, BY SUCCEEDING.'

MICHAEL TURNER (*TRUTH*, 1988)

———•———

# 16 STAND UP AND
# BE COUNTED

Sydney's Roddy Carter was a tough old bastard. He used to stand on my toes, stick his bony elbows into me and generally try to drive me crazy.

He was a real, honest goer, not overblessed with ability or anything. But he'd give 100 per cent every week and that's all you can ask from anyone.

I found I couldn't get rid of him, no matter what. He wouldn't go out and meet the player coming towards him. He was a bugger like that. If you could kick a couple on him early, I felt he lost a little bit of confidence. But if he beat you a couple of times early, he grew in stature and he was always going to be hard to beat for the rest of the day.

When opposed by him, I always tried to do something early to break his concentration. He taught me that you just can't afford to stand still and wrestle. I've never allowed myself to be pushed around by him or any other full back. That's the way it is and always will be with me. No matter who it is, you've got to stand up and be counted.

North Melbourne's Mick Martyn is in the Rod Carter mould. I've got a lot of respect for him. I can see us having some really good afternoons together. All Mick Martyn wants to do is to annoy you and climb all over you. He'll do it all day if you let him. He's a pretty hardened sort of campaigner and I rate him. Sometimes our meetings have got a little bit heated. But that's natural. I'm trying to kick goals and he's trying to stop me. At Moorabbin in 1991, I didn't intend to be pushed around and I don't think he did either. Everything pointed to a heated exchange. It was going to happen sometime, whether it was

A bit of a push and shove with Steve O'Dwyer and Jim Stynes, Moorabbin, 1988.
I've never allowed myself to be pushed around.

in the first quarter or after the game. I think it will go on
happening too. I was pretty steamed up before Stewie Loewe
dragged me out of that one. The best way I know to hurt a
bloke is to kick a heap of goals on him.

That's what I keep telling myself anyway. The bigger the
scoreline, the more demoralised they get.

# 17 A LIFE-LONG CONTRACT

Money is very important in football. Those who say it isn't are kidding themselves. You're entitled to look after yourself as your time in football is short.

If you're a high-money earner, you've got to be able to put that money to work and use it properly. When the time comes and you're not playing footy any more, it's good to know that you have been able to set yourself up.

My first contract at St Kilda was for $300 a senior game and $200 if I played in the reserves. It was an unbelievable amount of money for a 17-year-old to be earning. There were built-in bonuses, too—something like $1000 for the first senior game and $1000 for the tenth game. It seems so long ago now.

At the time when they came to me with the proposal, I was still training in Ballarat and earning $20 a win and $10 a loss. Mum still has a photostat of my first-ever footy cheque at home.

Dad did most of the early negotiating on my behalf. Ian Stewart (St Kilda's general manager and triple Brownlow Medallist), told Dad that young players had to serve an apprenticeship and there would be more money later. When Dad told me I was to get $300 a game, I was over the moon.

There had been a few nibbles from other clubs, but never directly to me. Collingwood were said to be keen at one stage* but I was out of all the talks and as far as money goes, I just don't know what figures were being tossed around.

* Late in the 1984 season, it was reported that Collingwood had offered Lockett, then eighteen, a three-year contract worth $20,000. Richmond was another club apparently keen, going after Lockett and another Ballarat-based player, Darryl Cunningham.

My first ever pay cheque, $20, from North Ballarat.

At the time, one of my cousins was going out with someone who worked at Collingwood. Apparently the club was keen to talk to me. But I was too young to worry about it and never got to a stage where I sat down with anyone from Collingwood.

Clubs have to be careful about the way they approach other teams' players. The offers came through my father or someone else close.

Currently I'm on a five-year contract which will see me through to when I'm about thirty. I'm pretty happy with it. I get paid each month, the money going straight into the bank. If I need some, I take it out. If I don't it just stays there. In 1992, I've got another two years to go.

It's performance-based, just like every player at St Kilda— incentives based around team performance. I don't get any extra money on the goals I kick. Everything is team-orientated. There are some bonuses involved, revolving around the number of games played. If I'm suspended or miss matches with injury, I risk losing a certain amount of bonus money.

It's a good enough deal, probably as good as anyone has ever got. Even if I wasn't getting the money I do out of the game, I think I'd be playing somewhere, probably back home, perhaps in Queensland. I just don't know. I've always loved the game for its own sake, and always will.

# 18 JOBS FOR THE BOY

When I first got to Melbourne, the club organised a job in a nursery for me. No-one said I had to have any experience. I lasted exactly one day, not that I didn't have a green thumb, mind you. I just didn't know the difference between a weed and a wallflower.

Next, I became a brickies' labourer. That lasted six weeks. 'What about sales repping?' the club suggested. But that didn't work either. I sold about one tin of auto paint in three months. I'd like to think I wasn't sacked. My leaving was mutually agreed.

After being a groundsman at the footy club for twelve months, I had a stretch working with Trevor Barker as a maintenance man at the King Club. I also did deliveries and general store work with Kids Biz Toys and Jumbo Toys. About the only thing I haven't done is sell pots and pans, like Simon O'Donnell.

Now, I'm into the greyhounds and loving it. It's what I like and what I enjoy doing. In the last two or three years I've become really serious about it.

From about the age of fourteen, I worked at the Ballarat dog track as a catcher. I'd earn a couple of dollars each race. If you were lucky and 'your' dog had won, you sometimes got a fiver. It was just pocket money, but other than a paper round, it was my first regular job.

As kids, we always had a pet dog, as well as cats, budgies and canaries. I also had a brown and white pony called Toby and used to love riding him. But I soon realised I was never going to be another Darren Gauci or anything like that.

I like any animal. I find them fascinating. Sometimes they're more honest than people. You know where you stand with most of them anyway.

About the only thing I haven't done is sell pots and pans . . . or been a cameraman!

I've owned dogs for the last five or six years and for the last two have trained them myself, along with my friend Darren McDonald, who runs the show when I am away with football.

In the season, my football commitments keep me away nearly every night. Saturdays are out and with interstate trips, you're away between one and three days.

Darren and I try to do everything together, training the dogs the same and looking after them identically. I'm very lucky to have someone who is as honest and as trustworthy.

We have eight dogs in work at the moment between us. I haven't as yet got a classic winner, just your normal races around the country. Before Christmas, Wild Scene won at Olympic Park which was a big thrill, and three of our dogs won in the same night in various country meetings in February.

Darren's had a third in the Melbourne Cup and third in the Australian Cup. We're both persevering, hoping that if we work hard enough for long enough and keep on learning, something will come of it.

To have one of your dogs win really means something, especially if you've had a lot to do with that dog from the breeding and rearing stages, right through to training.

Top: I like any animal. I find them fascinating. Darren and I with some of our dogs, from left: Grumpy, Smokey, Mouse, Flipper and Spicy. If we called them by their racing names, they wouldn't know who we were talking to!

Bottom: Darren and I with Black Pirate.

I get a great buzz out of going to the dogs and seeing any of ours doing well. It doesn't matter to me whether the dogs win at Albury, Sale or a little country track. A win is a win in my book and you place your dogs where you think they can win.

Whatever I've tried in my life I've always tried to be successful at it. I'd love one of my dogs to win a couple of classic races. There are only one or two people who can do that each year though. If your number comes up, well and good. That's what everyone is striving for.

My interest in the dogs is not just a hobby, it's something I'm going to try to make a livelihood out of in the years to come.

I'm learning gradually and realise that success doesn't come immediately with anything you do. We have a good set-up on two-and-a-half acres out at Devon Meadows. We're surrounded by good people, several who also have dogs. It's also close to training.

# 19 I LOVE MY FOOD –
## BUT NEVER ON SATURDAYS

I can't eat before a game. The dietitians may not like it, but that's just the way it is. I don't follow a set Friday night meal plan either. I might have spaghetti or a steak and vegies. It doesn't matter much. Whatever it is, I always eat around 7 p.m.

Sometimes I go out and do a bit of shopping, just to keep myself active and my mind off the game or I stay in and watch a video.

On match days, I follow the same low key routine, trying to remain as relaxed as possible. I usually sleep in to about 10 a.m., before having a bit of a walk around outside. I have a cup of coffee and maybe a few glasses of water but nothing else.

I generally sit down and take it easy until about 11.15 when I go and have a shower, get my gear on and leave about 11.30. Darren looks after all the dogs for me on Saturdays. I only have to worry about myself.

If we're playing at Moorabbin, we all have to be at the ground by 12.30 p.m. I make sure when I get to the rooms and get stripped that I have time to handle the ball for about five minutes. I have a few kicks and take a few marks. When I feel comfortable, I stop.

I like to have a quick look at the reserves before going into the team meeting at 12.45 p.m.

I'm usually first out of the door afterwards, so I can get my ankles taped when there's no-one else in the medical room. Kenny Whiffen looks after me. He invariably tapes my ankles on training nights and on match days. Kenny's a bit of a legend around the place, having been club runner in the 1966 Grand

Final and around for every year since. He always rubs Deep Heat or something else like that into my bad ankle, just to warm it up a bit.

For my asthma, there's a nebuliser machine that quite a few of us get on before the game. We sit in the medical room for five minutes with face masks on. Sometimes I have to use the Ventolin spray before the match, at quarter-time and at half-time. There have been times when I have lost my breath completely and been really gone during a game.

Before going out I must also have my customary spew—it wouldn't feel right if I didn't. The trainers usually have a bin in there ready for me when the coach is talking. That's why I can't have anything to eat on a Saturday morning. It's usually just a bit of saliva and biley stuff that comes out. If I had any food, I know I'd be in trouble.

I also have a shot of local anaesthetic to ease the pain in my groin. I've tried to rest it but it never seems to fully recover. It's something I just have to put up with.

Running out onto the ground, I'm invariably second in line behind Danny Frawley. But I rarely stay there! It all depends. If I feel really good, I'm up there. Usually, though, I'm a bit lethargic and sluggish at first. Those first few run-throughs are always really hard.

When we finish our lap and our few run-throughs and the balls come out, I go straight over to the trainers and have a real good whiff of the Ventolin and the smelling salts. They blow your eyes out for a while, but it's just what I do. I have a little bit of a kick and I'm ready to go.

# 20 LOST WEEKEND

Saturday, 6 May 1989. It's a day I remember well, for all the wrong reasons. We played Sydney at home and won. I wasn't outstanding, but still kicked six goals to have 43 in the opening six matches of the season.

We moved to within a game of the top five and that night I stayed in the social club later than normal. Having lost my licence for a month*, I knew I wasn't driving so I let my hair down a bit.

Talking footy late at night when men have got too many beers in them invariably promotes arguments. Someone who should have known better told me how I should have kicked more than six goals and basically accused me of not doing enough. I got wilder and wilder as he spoke. And things which shouldn't have happened, happened.

There was a bit of a push and shove. Rick Watt, our general manager, was in the wrong place at the wrong time. I put him on his backside but he was all right. He got up.

I know it shouldn't have happened. But it did. I was pretty angry. Later I apologised to Rick. I have no beef with him or him with me. After the blue I left the club with my brother and a mate, who was driving.

On the way home, we must all have fallen asleep because when we woke up, we had run off the side of the road and were bogged.

We hailed down a driver who got some help and we were towed out. By the time I got to bed, it was 5.30 a.m.

* He'd been booked for doing 142 kmh in a 100 kmh zone at Rockbank between Melton and Melbourne.

State training was on at 8 a.m. and I set the alarm, fully intending to get up and get there.

When it went off, all the happenings of the night before flashed into my mind. I remembered hitting Rick and knew everyone had seen it. I knew there'd be people waiting to hound me at training. I didn't feel too flash, so turned over and went back to sleep and didn't wake up again until 3 p.m.

Unbeknown to me, Ted Whitten, the Victorian chairman of selectors, had gone on television and blasted me for not turning up.

The heat intensified when news of the social club scuffle broke out. It was a bad time for me. But several weeks later, things were to get even hotter.

---

'IT WOULD BE A TRAGEDY, NOT ONLY FOR ST KILDA, BUT FOR FOOTBALL GENERALLY TO SUSPEND TONY LOCKETT FROM THIS WEEK'S GAME AGAINST GEELONG. HIS "CRIME" IS TO HAVE MISSED STATE TRAINING. BIG DEAL! IF THE VFL RUBS OUT A CROWD-PULLER JUST FOR THAT, IT WILL LOSE THOUSANDS OF SUPPORTERS.'

JOHN RICE (*TRUTH*, 1989)

---

# 21 THE GUY McKENNA
## INCIDENT

That 1989 season was going to be my best year, despite the social club flare-up and the controversy over my non-appearance at State training which ended up costing me a $1500 fine.

I had 58 goals in eight games and in the ninth round at Moorabbin, booted twelve against the Eagles, equalling my personal best. Unfortunately, that day I also went on report, on a charge of striking Guy McKenna.

The rest is history and for me, so was my season.* I never really recovered after that enforced lay-off. My form went downhill. I was injured and played only two more club matches, plus one for Victoria.

I still say to this day that I didn't really hit McKenna that hard. The whistle had blown and I had the ball. I wasn't playing on or anything like that. Perhaps he didn't hear the whistle. I don't know. But he continued to apply a tackle.

All I tried to do was shrug him off—get him to let go of my jumper. He went down, apparently concussed, but at the time I thought he might have been laying it on a bit too.

The West Coast blokes jumped in, telling field umpire Michael Sneddon to report me. It all heated up, with their blokes retaliating. I came back at them and after it all stopped, I was reported. I guess I was a bit unlucky.

I don't think he was going to report me to start with, because he didn't take my number until about a minute after everything had died down.

They held the tribunal the next morning and found me guilty.

---

* I received four weeks' suspension, my heaviest tribunal sentence.

The whistle had blown and I had the ball. I wasn't playing on or anything like that.

Top: All I tried to do was shrug him off . . .

Bottom: The West Coast blokes jumped in, telling field umpire Michael Sneddon to report me.

Suddenly I had a month cooling my heels.

My earlier disqualifications were taken into account and suddenly I had a month cooling my heels. St Kilda tried to get the case re-heard, but had no luck.

I was savage, especially after Carlton's Justin Madden did the same thing the following week and no-one said a word.

I never really recovered from the suspension. Neither did the team. From being just on the outskirts of the five, we won only two more games for the entire year to finish twelfth.

---

'I'VE NEVER SEEN A FOOTBALLER CAST A SPELL ON THE CROWD AS TONY LOCKETT DID AGAINST US AT MOORABBIN. IT WAS AMAZING TO SEE A WAVE OF PEOPLE MOVE AFTER EACH QUARTER TO LOCKETT'S GOAL-SCORING END.'

JOHN TODD, COACH OF THE WEST COAST EAGLES (*INSIDE FOOTBALL*, 1989)

---

# 22 OVERSTEPPING THE MARK

The worst thing about being in the public eye so much is that you're recognised everywhere you go. And, unfortunately, wherever you go there's always going to be a yahoo. Sometimes they probably get the better of me.

It's very hard to put up with people all the time. There was an incident in Tasmania which at the time was pretty serious, and for a while there people were saying I wouldn't be allowed to go back there.

Sometimes a few smart-arses want to have their two bobs' worth. Sometimes I get a little bit sick of it and let off a bit of steam.

But there's nothing worse than going out and being hounded all night. I'm the same as everyone else. I like to go out with my friends. I'm not out to cause any trouble or anything like that. I'm just out to have a good time like everyone else.

I've overstepped the mark a few times but I'm sure just about everyone has. We're all only human and have our limitations. Some have more limitations than others.

I've stepped over the line a few times, but I regret little that I've done. I do what I think is right at the time. I live by that attitude. It's either hit or be hit.

I guess I blame half of what happened in Tasmania on myself. I shouldn't have been in that nightclub in Hobart after midnight. I was asking for trouble. We'd all had a bit to drink. There was a fight and I was in it.

The aftermath was that someone said I should be arrested if I ever came to Tasmania again. Thankfully, that was all sorted out.

It would have been terrible if we'd been drawn to play over there and I wasn't able to take my place in the team.

I admit I made a mistake that night and on other occasions too. It all stems back to the privacy bit. How would you like it if people kept on coming up to you and asking for an autograph while you're in the middle of your dinner? I don't like it and never will.

I used to go out a lot. The nightclubs in Ballarat were all right; Hot Gossip, Power Station and the Canopy Club. They were all good fun. There was probably less trouble in those clubs because everyone knew me and left me alone. Often I'd go with Vicki, Danny Frawley and his fiancée (now his wife) Anita.

It was a big step coming from there to the nightclubs in Melbourne. They were completely different from what I was used to. Now I stop at home more. Video recorders are a great invention.

# 23 FUN WITH WILLO,

## SPUD AND BURNSEY

Brian Wilson is the funniest man I've ever run into at a footy club. 'Willo' wasn't happy unless he was playing a joke on someone. He never played one on me, but Danny Frawley, Stewie Loewe and Willo were forever trying to outdo each other.

I was lucky to spend a couple of nights boarding with him on our interstate trips in 1991. Even though he lasted less than a year with us, he was hilarious company and a good bloke to boot.

He'd been up to all sorts of pranks with 'Spudda' Frawley and Stewie and one day they hit back, supergluing his wipers to the windshield on his Porsche, just before heavy rain set in for the night.

Of course he couldn't get his wipers going and ended up burning the wiper motor out. It cost him $850 to fix. He didn't think it was much of a joke at the time but after a week or two, realised he probably got his fair whack back.

Frawley never admitted he was the culprit, but it's an open secret who did it. What got Frawley's back up was the night Willo planted some tiny, harmless white mice in Danny's tracksuit pants. Danny came in after training, had a shower, put his pants on and felt something wriggling in his pocket. Just as he looked down, Willo yelled: 'Snake, snake!'

I'll never forget it. I've never seen a bloke get his strides off so quickly! He was just about airborne as he ripped them off. The boys had all been tipped off and were roaring with laughter. Spud saw the mice and went to grab Willo by the throat before he saw the funny side of it.

He may be serious here, but Brian Wilson is the funniest bloke I've ever run into at a footy club.

Willo tried the same trick on Stewie, too. It worked a beauty, but it could have been a bit dangerous. Stewie felt a wriggle in his tracksuit pants as he was driving home one night. He was on a roundabout and in his panic, slammed on his brakes and a car hit him from behind. No-one was hurt, but Willo was overwhelmed with the success of it all.

Mark Jackson also loved a practical joke. At Lorne during a

training camp, he put a brick under Trevor Barker's brake pedal. Luckily 'Barks' found out while he was still in the carpark. Another of Jacko's party tricks was to plant lighted cigarettes in the pocket of anyone whose back was turned.

We stayed at the Lorne surf life-saving club once, and Jacko kept us awake all night rolling billiard balls up and down the old, wooden floorboards.

That was the trip when Con Gorizidis refused to get out of bed to join the boys for a 6 a.m. run. We'd all had a huge night and Con just refused to budge. Tony Jewell called him every name under the sun. He had steam coming out of his nostrils in the end, but all to no avail. Needless to say, Con wasn't with us for too much longer.

Spudda Frawley, Greg Burns and I used to drive down from Ballarat to Moorabbin for training.

One year we nearly sent a market gardener in Bacchus Marsh out of business. Just for fun, we used to pull up on the side of the road on the way home from training, hop the fence and load up Burnsey's big Nissan Patrol with pumpkins and whatever else was on offer.

This went on for quite a while, the 'proceeds' being distributed around the families of the district.

One night, instead of getting a couple of pumpkins each— our usual haul— we filled up the back of the car with about 25 pumpkins, all a good 18–24 cm across. They were whoppers. On the way home, the front wheels were barely hitting the ground, with all the pumpkins, and we ended up having a puncture.

As we were putting the spare tyre on, a policeman came up behind us and asked: 'Is everything all right, gentlemen?'

'Yeah. We've just got a bit of a flat tyre.'

'What have you got in the back there?' he asked.

'Oh, just a few pumpkins.'

'Aren't you footballers from St Kilda?'

'Yeah.'

'How come you've got all these pumpkins?'

'We've been to Victoria Market.'

Soon afterwards, the farmer put up an electric fence, which immediately ended our activities.

I was half-way across one night when I got the old tingling sensation in a rather sensitive place. The boys thought it was terrific. I smile about it now. But back then, it was agonising!

Another night Burnsey brought his brother-in-law, a shop proprietor from Snake Valley, down to training. He'd called into

Three of my best mates from footy: 'Spud' Frawley, Trevor Barker and Greg Burns, the Buckrat.

the Egg Board on the way to get a heap of eggs for his shop.

Spudda and I went back with them as usual, putting our feet up in the back of his 4-wheel drive, in readiness for the long trip home.

This time, though, we were surrounded by all those eggs. Talk about a temptation! I winked at Spud and away we went, taking great pleasure in pinging them at anything and everything from Linton St, South Rd, all the way around Beach Rd to the Westgate freeway.

One poor bloke was waiting out the front of his office for a ride and Spud and I hung out the back window and fired about six eggs at him. They all missed, and he gave us the two fingers, so we did a U-turn, turned back and gave it to him again. Burnsey had caught on to what was happening and couldn't resist it. He's a real kid at heart.

Most training nights Burnsey would pick me up from the bottle shop at the Cattle Yards Inn, where I used to work, go and get Danny and head off to Melbourne.

Just before Spud's house, we noticed that his father had knocked off a sheep. He had it hanging in a tree. On the way home that night, we dropped Spud off, went up the road a little bit further where the sheep was hanging and we took it home.

Roddy Owen: I've never seen a bloke sober up quicker.

We chopped it all up nicely and had a heap of chops and roasts.

Getting to Spud's house on the Thursday night, we found out that Mr Frawley had rung the Bungaree police and a big search party was out after this bloody sheep carcass. The farmers around the district were a bit worried about people going around knocking their things off. There was a big commotion over it. Danny knew what had happened, though. He didn't let us forget it for twelve months!

In the end, we replaced the carcass, buying one from the butcher's shop. But the 'replacement' was nowhere near as good as the original.

Burnsey had a team of trotters, including Trudi's Gold which won quite a few races—much to Roddy Owen's delight, who'd backed it from the outset.

One day Roddy said to Burnsey how he wanted to come up and see the 'wonder' horse which was keeping his TAB phone account profitable. It was decided we'd have an 'Easter Classic' out at Burnsey's house and even teed up someone to videotape the big race.

There were about eight horses in the field, Burnsey, Spud, myself and Roddy being among the drivers. Roddy had put in a huge night in Ballarat the night before. I don't think he'd ventured into the kipper at all and on arrival was still blowing the breathalyser apart.

Burnsey's ears pricked on hearing that Roddy, a city slicker, had never been near a horse before. Pointing Roddy in the direction of 'a nice, quiet thing', he helped him into the rig.

Almost immediately, the horse bolted and Roddy couldn't stop it. It was the quickest I'd ever seen a bloke sober up. This thing went around and around the track until it finally exhausted itself.

The entertainment over, we went into our race, minus one R. Owen, who was stretched out somewhere, trying to recover. Burnsey tried to fix me with one of the slower horses, but after a great tactical race, I ran second. Burnsey was quite impressed. 'There might be a future for you as a trotting driver later on,' he winked. 'If you can take off about five stone!'

# 24 ADDICTED TO
## FAST FOOD

Trevor Barker reckons that when I shifted down from Ballarat, the local fast food industry was devastated. He said a string of takeaway shops in between Melbourne to Ballarat went bust. He still uses the gag at sportsmen's nights. But I don't mind, I'm usually sitting next to him.

I admit to being big on the old takeaways, but:

- I've never ever in my life eaten a family sized pizza. I can just get through a medium;
- I don't classify myself as a really big eater. I'm a lot wiser these days about my fitness and the foods I should be eating.

I know how hard it is come January to have to shed 10 kilograms and get back into reasonable nick. I was kidding myself trying to do that, but I guess I was one for the good times too.

After a long, hard, pressure-packed year at football, I liked to get away from it all and really let my hair down.

Now, as soon as the season is over, I virtually diet right through summer until we start training.

Some blokes at the club lose weight because they stop training. They must have incredible metabolisms. Nicky Winmar appears able to eat and drink what he likes, yet is invariably lean and super-fit.

---

'LOCKETT IS OBVIOUSLY ONE OF THOSE UNFORTUNATE PEOPLE WHO COULD PUT ON A KILO JUST BY THINKING ABOUT STUFF LIKE POTATOES, BREAD AND EASTER EGGS!'

RON BARASSI (*TRUTH*, 1985)

---

93

The dietitians at the club have helped me a lot but in the long run, it really gets down to how much you want to help yourself. I try to eat the right things and in the off-season, have a jog every couple of days to get a bit of sweat up.

If you work hard pre-season, your body becomes used to the heavy workload. I used to stop all of a sudden, but keep consuming the same amount of food, and my weight would balloon.

---

'TONY LOCKETT IS DEFINITELY OVERWEIGHT (BY 3.5 KG)—BY HIS OWN ADMISSION, DIRECT TO TED WHITTEN AND MYSELF AND EVEN MORE BY SCALES TAKEN OUT TO STATE TRAINING LAST WEEK. THE SELECTORS HAVE EXPRESSED A DESIRE THAT WE WANT ONLY COMMITTED PLAYERS.'

STATE SELECTOR RON BARASSI, EXPLAINING LOCKETT'S ABSENCE FROM VICTORIA'S TEAM FOR

THE BICENTENARY CARNIVAL (*TRUTH*, 1988)

---

I always knew I was going to be big but I didn't think I was going to turn out to be as big as I am today.

My problem, especially in my late teen years, was that I ate the wrong foods. My diet wasn't balanced. I never used to eat any fruit, just takeaways. I was hopeless. I was a big takeaway food addict, mainly because it was a lot more convenient than having to cook for yourself. It was easier to go down the street and get a heap of takeaway. I guess it was my biggest killer.

Looking back on it now, that was the habit which I probably should have changed. But, it was part of growing up.

As a young kid my fitness came naturally, but the older I get, especially now that I'm 26, I realise how hard I must work my body. The need to control my weight has been compounded by my asthma condition, which first flared when I was about fourteen or fifteen. Before then, I'd been as good as gold; I was as fit and healthy as any young kid. The doctors said it was hereditary but neither my Mum and Dad nor my sisters or brother suffer from it. But one of my little cousins does. She's only three.

As I've got older it's got a little bit worse too, making it harder to get fit.

# 25 MY MOST
## SATISFYING GOALS

A lot of people ask me if any one goal stands out ahead of another. When you've played for ten years, that is a mighty difficult question to answer.

I won 'Goal of the Year' in 1987 for a long boomerang against Footscray, but I have only faint recollections of it.

One which does sit in my memory though was against Fitzroy in Hobart in mid-year, 1991. I was in a marking contest, lost it, but followed it up and had a flying ping over my shoulder from about fifty metres. There was a fair amount of luck involved. If it had spun normally, it would have been a behind. But it held up a little and the wind got hold of it just at the right time and helped it through post-high. It was probably as good a goal as any I've kicked.

The Melbourne game in early 1987 when I kicked twelve goals* also stands out. But we lost, so it didn't mean much.

Kicking ten against Carlton in early 1989 was very exciting. I was off-target, kicking something like seven or eight points, too. But we won by four points in an exciting finish. One reporter asked me later if I was a one-man team. I wasn't that impressed. Without the others supplying me with the ball, who was I? Nothing.

Any of the games that you kick up around elevens and twelves is pretty satisfying. But winning days are always better than losing ones. In 1991, I kicked thirteen against Carlton, which was my personal best and a new club record.

---

* He kicked twelve out of a team score of fourteen goals. It was the first time Lockett had kicked a double figure score.

Top: My best return in an opening round of the season: ten against Footscray at the Western Oval, 1990. Pictured with me is Roo-turned-Bulldog Tim Harrington, who I'd opposed in my very first game for St Kilda—back in 1983.

Bottom: Yes, it's through and we win by four points, with about 34 seconds to go! My tenth against Carlton, round two, Moorabbin, 1989.

On the way to twelve against the Eagles, Moorabbin, 1989. I was particularly happy with this one. I'd lost a boot only seconds before.

I was told that no-one had ever before kicked six lots of ten or more goals in the same season, but our win/loss record* was more important to me. My job is to kick goals and hopefully I can continue for some time yet. Any goal gives me satisfaction. It's six points the opposition has to make up.

## TONY LOCKETT'S 'BIG BAGS'

| GOALS | AGAINST | ROUND | GROUND |
|---|---|---|---|
| 15 | Sydney Swans | R 13, 1992 | Moorabbin |
| 13 | Carlton | R 21, 1991 | Waverley Park |
| 12 | Brisbane Bears | R 10, 1992 | Moorabbin |
| 12 | Adelaide Crows | R 7, 1991 | Moorabbin |
| 12 | Sydney Swans | R 9, 1991 | Sydney |
| 12 | West Coast Eagles | R 9, 1989 | Moorabbin |
| 12 | Melbourne | R 4, 1987 | MCG |
| 11 | Sydney | R 24, 1991 | Moorabbin |
| 10 | Carlton | R 2, 1989 | Moorabbin |
| 10 | Footscray | R 1, 1990 | Western Oval |
| 10 | Brisbane | R 8, 1991 | Carrara |
| 10 | Adelaide Crows | R 22, 1991 | Football Park |
| 10 | Adelaide Crows | R 7, 1992 | Moorabbin |

* Fourteen wins, seven losses and one tie, which enabled St Kilda to take fourth position coming into the finals, their highest home-and-away finish since 1972 when they also came fourth. In 1973, they were fifth.

# 26 MEMO
## BIG BROTHER

Sometimes I wonder if those who control the game care what the players think. I reckon they'd have us playing virtually every day of the week if they could. The game is rapidly becoming over-exposed and is in danger of losing its identity. If there's too much footy, the playing spans of leading players must be affected.

The television rights appear all-important. I don't reckon some administrators care two hoots about the players.

Once upon a time, not so long ago, Saturday was football day. To me, that was great.

As it is, now, you have to constantly change all your training schedules around to play on Sundays, sometimes Mondays, and even mid-week. Easter Monday is a killer. I don't enjoy that at all. We had to play on Easter Monday in 1991 and it happened again in 1992.

Perhaps we'll draw a Saturday match come Easter, 1993.

# KEEP STATE FOOTBALL
## FOR SATURDAYS

**27**

I have a firm policy about State football. I won't risk myself for Victoria if it means St Kilda loses out. St Kilda is where my future is. They pay me and I return their loyalty by doing my best for them.

State games only come along a couple of times a year, whereas we play anything from 22 to 26 official games at club level.

My priorities are to the club and always will be. Money doesn't come into it. What's got to be done with State football is this: instead of playing mid-week fixtures on a Tuesday or Wednesday and asking blokes to front up again for club footy on the Saturday, the State match should take the place of a weekend round.

The State match should be played on a Saturday, as happened in 1989, when Victoria met South Australia at the MCG. The crowd loved it; more than 90,000 went and that was after weeks of rain and when the ground was at its heaviest.

It's ridiculous to expect State players to front up for three matches in seven or eight days. By playing on a Saturday, blokes have a chance to recover from niggly little injuries before the next club game.

The ones most affected are the blokes who play around the middle or on the ball. They're the ones with the extra heavy workloads. It's not so bad for someone like me, playing a set spot at one end of the ground.

But no matter who you are, if you get injured in one of these games, or if you carry an injury and make it worse, you risk missing three or four of your own club games. That's when you really get disappointed and your club is entitled to ask why.

More than 90,000 packed the MCG for that 1989 State game. The crowd loved it. So did we!

The administrators should really look at State football and say there's a time and a place for it—at the weekend.

Everyone enjoys playing the games, but I bet if you did a survey and asked the players what they really wanted, most of the guys wouldn't play, especially if the State games continued to be scheduled mid-week.

The 1989 State-of-Origin match in Melbourne between S.A. and Victoria attracted such a good crowd that I was surprised State matches weren't immediately scheduled in Melbourne each year.

As it was, it took until May 1992 for another interstate game to be played, against the West Aussies. I reckon there's nothing worse than having to travel to Perth and Adelaide for State games all the time. The games should be set up on a round robin basis, with one match at home and one match away each year. And scheduling them mid-season is the go. For a few years, they played the games at the end of the season, but it wasn't a success.

The seasons are long enough now, especially with the night games starting early in February. Until the start of 1992, I'd played

101

just three State games, missed selection in several and been unavailable, through injury, for many others.*

Last year I carried niggly injuries through the season and couldn't see the sense in fronting up and playing extra games and putting extra pressure on myself to perform. If things turned out for the worse and made my injuries worse, I was going to be in trouble at St Kilda.

My main objective was to do my best for the footy club and make sure we got into the finals. That was all I wanted. I didn't care about anything else. I just wanted to front up each Saturday and put in an effort that would see us reach the finals. And now we've had a taste, we want more.

* I played in 1985 v W.A. (Perth), in 1987 v S.A. (Adelaide) and in 1989 v S.A. (Melbourne).

# 28 AN UNFORGETTABLE EXPERIENCE

While I'm happiest playing club football for St Kilda, I must say that the 1989 State game at the MCG between Victoria and South Australia was an unforgettable experience.

It was as good a highlight as you'd ever get—other than, I suppose, a Grand Final. I've never played in front of a crowd like that before (91,960), especially when they were virtually all barracking for one team: Victoria.

I was pleased with my effort—I got five goals to three-quarter time—but the ground was very heavy and I hurt my groin, the start of some long-running injury problems for me.

I'd been out for five weeks and leading up to the game hadn't trained much. I went on this orange diet I'd seen written up in a magazine. You were supposed to lose 10 kg in three days by eating 12 oranges a day. You weren't allowed to have anything else, bar a thin slice of cheese with each serving.

I lasted about a day and three quarters before I finally cracked and hoed into something substantial. I can't remember what it was, it disappeared too fast!

Still, I lost four or five kg, helped by the daily training sessions I was doing with Tony 'Shep' Royden at Bacchus Marsh. Because my condition had fallen away in the first three weeks of my suspension, I knew I was underdone going into the game and I was reluctant to play. But there was a lot of pressure on me to make myself available. I thought I'd be letting everyone down if I pulled out. Then again, not having played for so long, I wondered what benefit I could be to the team.

Once I was named in the side though, I was keen to do well. I had a bit of a chat to the others beforehand on how

103

# VICTORIA
## COACH: BILL GOGGIN

| | G | B |
|---|---|---|
| 1—Simon Madden (C) | | |
| 2—Dale Weightman (VC) | | |
| 3—Paul Couch | | |
| 4—Andrew Collins | | |
| 5—David Murphy | | |
| 6—Barry Mitchell | | |
| 8—Robert Scott | | |
| 9—Gavin Brown | | |
| 10—Neville Bruns | | |
| 11—Darrin Pritchard | | |
| 12—Sean Wight | | |
| 13—Andrew Bews | | |
| 14—Tim Watson | | |
| 15—Brett Lovett | | |
| 16—Shane Morwood | | |
| 17—Tim Darcy | | |
| 18—Barry Stoneham | | |
| 19—Jason Dunstall | | |
| 21—Terry Daniher | | |
| 22—Garry Lyon | | |
| 23—Dermott Brereton | | |
| 24—Chris Langford | | |
| 25—Greg Dear | | |
| 26—Tony Lockett | | |
| *Rushed* | | |

We fielded a star-studded side . . .

I was going to play the position—I was to be full forward with Jason Dunstall in a pocket alongside—and how much it meant to me to be playing for the State, especially in Melbourne.*

There was almost a giant hiccup before the game. Ted Whitten came over and said to me: 'What boots are you wearing today Plugger, moulded soles or screw-ins? It's pretty wet out there. You'd better give me a look at them.' I searched in my bag and found I didn't have any boots at all! And starting time was just twenty minutes away!

* The 1989 State game between Victoria and S.A. was the first one scheduled for the Melbourne Cricket Ground since 1971.

The pre-game publicity included this front-page caricature of Johnny Platten and myself in *Inside Football*.

Suddenly Ted produced them. 'A bloke gave them to me outside.'*

'You footballers. You'd forget your head if it wasn't screwed on!' He's pretty right too. I've got a bad habit of forgetting things!

I was going to play only half a game, but everything was going well and I didn't feel too bad so I stayed on. While I was pretty tired, it was nice to be on the ground and involved. Jason played next to me and between us, we got nine goals and took something like twenty marks. Late in the game Dermott Brereton came on and killed them. Terry Daniher, Simon Madden and Gavin Brown also dominated.

---

* A friend of mine, Ian Flood, had driven all the way from Ballarat with the boots.

Jason Dunstall played next to me and between us, we got nine goals and took something like twenty marks.

Enjoying the victory spoils with Teddy Whitten. He's never let me forget about those 'missing' boots of mine!

Late in the game, I felt a bit of a twinge in my groin. The ground was really heavy that day and unfortunately my injury problems flared from there. I pulled up sore and could play only two more club matches before missing the rest of the season. Having sat out half a year in 1988, here I was doing it again in 1989. It was yet another frustrating time for me.

It was three years before I played for Victoria again and—you guessed it—I was hurt again. This time a wrenched shoulder kept me out for a fortnight and out of our big games against Geelong and Collingwood. After playing all year, suddenly I was sidelined again. It was agony.

Dermott Brereton came on and killed them.

# 29 TRAINING
# TORTURE

For the last two years, we've spent a summer weekend at Puckapunyal army camp, donning full gear and big boots and completing a variety of exercises.

The first time we were there, in the 1991 pre-season, they presented a real killer course, but none of the guys conceded. In 1992, it was designed differently and everyone split up into teams and had to help each other.

These camps are becoming popular and can be good if used the right way. They certainly give you variety and while I don't actually look forward to them, they beat the hell out of running 400-metre sprints around Moorabbin Oval in high summer.

I reckon I had nightmares for years after one pre-season, in 1983–84, when Terry Moore took us for training.

It was torture. I'd never known anything like it. We did an incredible amount of running. It must have been almost 40 degrees for our last session before Christmas. Terry's 'going-away present' was for us to do fifteen 400-metre sprints.

If you're not sure how tough that is, wait until a mid-summer's day and try two or three. Make sure you do them in seventy seconds and give yourself a maximum of seventy seconds rest in between.

---●---

'IF TONY LOCKETT STAYS FIT, PLAYS ALL 22 GAMES AND MELBOURNE REMAINS DRY THIS WINTER, THE MAGICAL 150-GOAL BARRIER WILL DEFINITELY BE BROKEN.'

COLLINGWOOD FULL FORWARD BRIAN TAYLOR (*SUNDAY HERALD*, 1989)

---●---

Puckapunyal the first time around: it was a real killer course.

I don't actually look forward to camps like these . . .

Anyway, that's what we had to do, running in groups of six or seven. As one group finished, the next would go and so on, until we'd all done fifteen.

It was probably the hardest training night I've ever put in, considering the heat. Not everyone got through it. I don't think I could now. I was the fittest I've ever been.

A few of the older blokes remember that training under Alex Jesaulenko was similarly arduous. His favourite was getting them to drag tractor tyres 40–50 metres before having them run at a swinging tackle bag! All I can say to that is that I'm glad I'm playing now, under Ken Sheldon and not under 'Jezza!'

# 30 RANDOM THOUGHTS...

## A SHORT WICK

I admit to having a short wick once. Young guys with inferiority complexes were forever wanting to have a go. There weren't too many places I could go without someone saying something. I didn't like that much. I still don't.

## BALLARAT AND BACK

Over the years, I've done thousands of miles driving to Melbourne and back for training and games.

I've gone through a few cars in my time, including three that were write-offs.

But driving backwards and forwards three and four times a week, for two hours each time, is something you get used to. I know that road backwards.

Anything is worthwhile if it means you make the finals, as happened to us in 1991.

## DIGGING FOR SPUDS

As part of my 'get fit quick' campaign in 1986, I took a job digging spuds at Danny Frawley's family farm in Bungaree. After working all day, Danny and I would go on these huge runs. It was part of my New Year's resolution to trim down and really give myself a chance. I lost 11 kg in five weeks.

## EXTRA SUPPORT

For a few weeks in 1984, I wore a wetsuit under my footy kit as my groin was playing up a little bit.

# Fitter, not fatter, Lockett meets Saints' challenge

Danny Frawley, an inspirational leader and a St Kilda man through and through.

I got there, Mike. Just.

It gave me extra support and kept the warmth around the injured area. But it was very uncomfortable and I was conscious of it when shooting for goal. After kicking 3.6 against Melbourne I got rid of it.

There are a lot of blokes doing it now, but the gear they wear is a lot lighter than it used to be.

I think Dermott Brereton started the trend, by wearing a pair of bright pink and green bike shorts one pre-season. These were unbelievable! I can still see his photo in the back of the paper, now.

## FINALS FEVER, 1992

Kenny Sheldon is dead set on not going back a step. He realises and we all realise how much work is required to get into the finals. That's got to be done again this year to enable us to make the finals, let alone finish fourth as in 1991.

Pre-season training was very hard and very serious. February and March are always the worst months of the year, as the games always seem so far away. Once you're into the proper season, it's great.

## GRAND FINAL LURE

This might sound strange, but I've only ever been to one Grand Final, in 1987, when I had to go and get my Brownlow. The

I was looking fairly fit—with Cameron O'Brien after our practice match with the Bears, at the start of 1989.

other times, I've just sat at home and watched it on the telly. I enjoy it more because you are in the comfort of your house and you can just do whatever you want. You do miss out on the atmosphere, but you don't get the hustle and bustle. I'm not really big at driving through all the traffic. That turns me off more than anything.

## HOME SWEET HOME

In my early years of League footy, I just wanted to come down, play the match and get back home again. Sometimes I even beat my Dad home on a Saturday.

I liked the idea of playing League footy, but I also liked the wide-open surroundings of Ballarat.

## JEZZA THE GENT

It was an honour before 1991's preliminary final to receive the John Coleman Medal from Alex Jesaulenko.

I'd been to a function at the Mulgrave club with Neil 'Coconut' Roberts in the morning and got over to the ground nice and early, thinking that the ceremony was on at half-time.

Mike Williamson was on the ground talking and suddenly he mentioned me, saying: 'And I don't know where the big fella is!'

I twigged what was going on and dashed down to the fence and onto the ground. Gary Stevens (Sydney) and Stephen Anderson (Collingwood) who had won the Morrish and Gardiner Medals were already there.

I was very apologetic to Mike and Jezza, but they didn't appear too worried. Jezza even held an umbrella over me as I spoke.

## JUST A FACE IN THE CROWD

If I'm not playing, I like going to the games just like everyone else. But when I do go, I usually like to sit away from everyone. You cop that much annoyance from people around the joint. Most people are well meaning, but having to answer the same question a hundred times about when you'll be back is no fun.

A slight hamstring injury put me out of our night game against Geelong earlier this year. I kept away from everyone and went right over to the other side of the ground. There was no fuss made of that.

Yet in 1989, when I was serving a suspension, people were having a go at me for not attending games. That was right at the time that I'd lost my licence, so it was harder than normal to get around, and then only through the help of friends. There were times I didn't go to the footy but there were other times when I was there, but people wouldn't even have known about that.

## LETTING THE OPPOSITION WORRY ABOUT ME

I'm not worried about anyone on the football field. My job is to kick goals, help us win and let the opposition worry about me.

Of course, I've had run-ins with blokes and paid the penalty. I'd like to think I can control my temper better these days.

## MANAGEMENT

Having a manager has been very helpful for me.

I have enough worries on my plate just getting out on the ground and playing to the best of my ability without having to worry about accounting matters, taxation and everything else.

Dandenong solicitor Robert Hession acts for me and everything is going fine.

Having someone handling these sorts of situations takes a bit of undue pressure off me.

## MEMO AUTOGRAPH HUNTERS...

I don't mind people asking me for an autograph or to pose for a picture.

The people love their footy that much and idolise the players and deserve some attention. Most of the time the player should stop, say hello and maybe sign an autograph. That is part and parcel of being a well-known footballer.

What I don't like is when people come up to me while I'm eating in a restaurant or a hotel.

I don't mind if they wait until afterwards, but not while I'm in the middle of a meal. Kids mightn't know any better—and I hardly ever knock them back—but their Mums and Dads should.

The only time I've ever knocked kids back is when there's been that many of them and I haven't had time to do them all. Maybe I could do ten, but not twenty. In cases like that it's better not to do any. I'm sure the kids will get me next time.

## MY FIRST FOOTY

Mum tells me I was about three when she bought me my first football, one of those brown, plastic ones. Apparently the dog eventually chewed it, but not before I'd kicked it against the fence so often, that the fence cracked!

## NOTHING'S IMPOSSIBLE, BUT...

Beating the record of 150 goals in a season* is not a motivating influence in my footy. I'm more interested in playing in successful St Kilda sides.*

However, I don't think the 150-goal mark is an impossible target. You would need things to be working in your favour to do it. Not many players kick more than eighty goals in a year. I would have to almost double that to break the record.

## PIE IN THE EYE

At first I wanted to play in the Bicentenary carnival in 1988, but the State selectors said I wasn't fit enough. I was automatically deleted out of their squad.†

They were right. I wasn't very fit. But who is in December and January?

I'd relaxed a bit after the Brownlow year. But I do every year.

Everyone needs two or three months off. I know I do anyway.

When the carnival was about to start, I kicked 12 goals against Brisbane in a practice match. The next day's papers had a picture of me walking off the oval with my jumper off. Underneath was the caption: 'Who says I'm too fat and not fit enough?'

It was a tongue-in-cheek comment, as actually the picture was OK. I was looking fairly fit.

It was pie-in-the-eye to the State selectors.

## PLUGGER SENIOR

My Dad goes to every game I play, no matter where it is: Perth, Carrara, wherever. He and Mum are my biggest fans.

## PROTECTION

Full backs can biff and scrag you and nothing will be done about it. But as soon as you do it back to them, the umpires are invariably on to you. I let them know what I think. Full forwards put up with a lot.

* The record held jointly by South Melbourne's Bob Pratt, in 1934, and Hawthorn's Peter Hudson, 1970.

† St Kilda's chief executive Keith Marshall was ropable at Lockett's omission from the Victorian side. He was quoted as saying: 'The fact that the reigning Brownlow Medallist and the top full forward is not in the side is amazing. I don't think it is that strong a side to leave out a player with his talent.'

Full backs can scrag and hold you and nothing will be done about it . . .

## READING THE PAPERS

I'm not a great reader of newspapers, though I look at the form guides and the sport on the back pages.

But I don't go down the street especially to buy a paper. Greyhound supplies yes, newspapers no!

Mum keeps all the scrapbooks of every year, but only pastes in the good stuff. All the bad press goes in a shopping bag. I don't get to see those!

## SCHOOLDAYS

I got into my fair share of strife at school, suspensions, letters home, bad reports, the lot.

I was all right at P.E., sports, woodwork and metalwork, but not much else.

119

# SHAWIE

A few people have asked me if Tony Shaw and I get on.

He plays for Collingwood and I play for St Kilda. That's the bottom line.

I respect the man as a footballer. He does his job. But there's no doubt the man has got a big mouth. But that's what he's there for.

He says a lot of things on the footy field which probably upset a lot of players. He's good at doing it. If he can do that and put a lot of players off, good luck to him.

If he's helping his side by putting a bloke off, or stopping him from kicking a goal, let him do it. They all have their different ways.

But I have no problems with him. Tony Shaw is Tony Shaw to me. He can be whatever he wants to be. It's not going to make any difference to me.

# SPORTSMEN'S NIGHTS

Trevor Barker and I team up and do a few through the footy season. We have a little routine going which is a bit of fun. He was a great player for St Kilda and this year for the first time, he is coaching, in the VFA with Sandringham.

# STARTING AT THE FIRST BOUNCE

I used to ruck a lot in my earlier days but haven't much at St Kilda except for a couple of games when Ken Sheldon started me at the first bounce, just for something different so I could have a bit of a run and warm up quickly.

I don't think there was a particular point to it other than to get me involved right from the start. It certainly didn't work to anyone's advantage. I went up in the ruck a few times but I don't think I got the tap even once.

The last time I rucked for any period of time was in the State match in Adelaide in 1987. We were getting beaten all night and at three-quarter time, Victorian coach Billy Goggin chucked me into the ruck for the last quarter. I don't know whether it fired the boys up a bit or whatever, but we came home with a wet sail and only just got beaten.*

* Victoria lost 12.13 (85) to 11.15 (81), Lockett having ten hit-outs, almost all in the last term when Victoria reduced a 22-point three-quarter time deficit to go down to South Australia by just four points.

Exchanging 'pleasantries' with Tony Shaw. I respect the man as a footballer, but . . .

Ruckwork: it's something different.

## TRUE BLUES

The support for St Kilda, especially for home games, never ceases to astonish me. That Moorabbin grandstand is always packed. People are very loyal and go to unbelievable lengths to show their support.

They get down there and watch training every night, rain, hail or shine. I reckon they'd just about die for their club. They're just so one-eyed and love the footy that much.

Sometimes they make so much noise in the grandstand that I wonder if it's going to fall down.

When the scores are pretty close and it's half-way through the last quarter, you can't help but be fired up with all the noise they make.

They have always been pretty true to me.

They have their fickle days and have been known to boo us off the ground—it has happened a few times—but perhaps the criticism was justified and we had let ourselves down.

## VICE-CAPTAIN OF ST KILDA

We were due to play Brisbane in a practice match at Carrara before the start of the 1987 season when I heard of my appointment as the club's deputy vice-captain.

Roddy Owen and I had teed up to room together but Doc Baldock split us up, getting me to go in with him, while Roddy got Allan Davis.

That night Doc asked me if I wanted to be deputy vice-captain of the club. It was a terrific honour for me and in 1988–89 I was vice-captain.

Now there's no formal vice-captain as such. All the senior players are leaders on the ground.

I did lead the side in a few early matches in 1992 when Danny Frawley had a groin injury. But I don't have any aspirations to captaining the club full time. Danny is a terrific leader and I can see him doing it for years to come. By the time he finishes, I'll be finished, too.

## WEAR AND TEAR

There are good and bad points about being so big. My ideal playing weight is around 103 kg. But the year I won the Brownlow, I finished up playing around 108 kg.

There's more wear and tear on my body than on somebody who plays at 80 kg. That's only natural.

You don't have to be a genius to work that out.

If I have a quiet day, invariably it's because the writers reckon I'm too big. You don't always win with the boys in the media!

## WHAT I REALLY THINK ABOUT WEIGHTWORK

I've done my fair share, but I'm naturally pretty strong anyway. I don't mind it for about twenty minutes. I do what I have to do and that's about it.

# Who says I'm too fat and not fit enough?

ST KILDA showed it is a genuine finals prospect with a comfortable 36-point win over he Brisbane Bears yesterday — but there is one ominous langer for the young Saints.

Total reliance on champion full-orward Tony Lockett could back-ire unless he maintains form week n, week out.

There will be days when Lockett loes not have it all his own way — ut if the Saints look to him as they lid in yesterday's practice match .t Moorabbin, then they have all he makings of a final five side.

The 1987 joint Brownlow Medal-ist was simply stunning.

He booted 12.7 out of St Kilda's ally of 20.19 (139).

His big hands fastened vice-like

*MICHAEL LOVETT watches the Saints outclass the Brisbane Bears*

# 31 SPUD FRAWLEY AND THE BEST PLAYERS OF MY TIME

Danny Frawley mightn't make too many Top 10 player lists, but he makes mine. He's the bloke I admire most in football. And he's been my toughest opponent, even if it is only during a Monday or Tuesday night match practice.

He's a genuinely hard man to play on. We're good mates, and I can't say we've ever had a real altercation, but it doesn't mean a thing when it comes to competing with each other. He'll throw me to the ground and vice versa in the man-on-man stuff.

Sometimes it gets very fiery, but we still respect each other. As soon as the session is finished, we pat each other on the back and we're good mates again.

Often we do a marking routine where we take it in turns in leading out from goal, one being the full forward and the other being the defender.

We always keep our score, too. He very rarely misses when going for goal. He may not be able to kick left foot, but he's nice and strong and very accurate on his right.

The idea of competitive work is to do it hard. If you don't, there's no use doing it. Danny is good to work with. He always works me hard.

It's the same on a Saturday. Very few of his opponents get the better of him.

Sometimes, our contests spread off the ground, too, to golf and tennis. One year I was picking spuds out at Frawley's farm and we got a bet going for the best of five tennis sets. We played the first set out at Frawley's home ground at Bungaree where there were plenty of weeds growing up near the white lines. We both cheated, calling things out when they were in and

125

Nicky Winmar: a magic player.

so on. It got a bit heated, racquets and swear words being freely thrown.

It was two sets all by the time we played the final in Bangkok during a trip away. I stayed with him for a while, but his fitness told in the end. He kept on running down balls and beat me, 3–2.

We've had a lot of fun together, from driving down to Moorabbin to spotlighting out the back of Ballarat. He's good fun and a good mate. He's also as good a leader as you'll find anywhere. I feel he'll captain the club until he's finished in four or five years' time. By then, I might be finished too.

Then the club may have to look at a young bloke like Robert Harvey or Nathan Burke to carry on and do the job for a long period. It's no good having the captaincy for just one or two years and handing it on.

A player like 'Harvs' has exceptional talent and while he is still very young, he has shown to everyone at St Kilda that

Robert Harvey: he's still young but has shown to everyone that he can be one of the greats.

127

he can be one of the greats. Harvs is still learning the game and if he maintains his improvement and dedication, he'll be phenomenal by the time he's 24 or 25.

He is rarely tackled and has remarkable balance, being able to keep his feet when others are slipping over all around him. He seems capable of running sideways, forwards and backwards, almost—if it was possible—in one motion. He's a terrific player and could be a sensation.

In time, he could rival the deeds of St Kilda's best player over the last fifteen years, the athletic Trevor Barker. Not only could Barks take a great mark and play at either end of the ground, he was also one of the best tacklers I've ever come across. Once he got his hands on you, that was it. He'd run you into the ground.

I know from personal experience, having often played against him at match practice in my early years. I'd have Barks, Harvs and Danny all in my Top 10 player list, with apologies to Nicky Winmar who is also a magic player.

The best player of my time virtually picks himself, the much-travelled Greg Williams. Before Williams signed with Carlton just before Christmas, 1991, it seemed for a few glorious days that he was Moorabbin-bound.

I know we were negotiating in a big way. In the end, we missed out. I wish we hadn't. It would have been fantastic to have had him, Harvs and Nicky Winmar all in the same side.

Williams is the best player I've seen in League football, bar none. Like Richmond's Dale Weightman, he has proved himself over many years. People say Williams lacks a yard in pace but he has terrific stamina and his ability to win the ball is unbelievable. He gets it as much as anyone in the game and what I particularly like about him is that he does something constructive with it every time.

There are a lot of players that can get the ball but none of them share it as expertly. Time after time, he'll hit his target, giving the opposition no chance of cutting it off.

Weightman is the same. He can handball 30 metres and pick out someone every time. He's machine-like in the way he plays.

He's also a tough and motivating leader who gets the ball at both ends of the ground—which isn't always the case with a rover. Everyone you talk to shares my admiration for him. And like everyone in my Top 10, he gives 100 per cent and is just about the ideal footballer.

Guys like Hawthorn's Leigh Matthews and Carlton's Bruce Doull were still magnificent players when I first started in 1983, even though both were into their 30s.

I only copped Doull at the end of his career, but I consider

There was nothing in this. Greg Williams is the best player I've seen, bar none.

Greg Williams almost came to us in 1992.

myself lucky to have played when he was playing. He was a great athlete, very cool and very professional. Whatever he did, he did it properly and to his team's advantage. Like all great players, he never ever wasted the ball. He would capitalise on every opportunity.

Matthews was an inspirational on-ball player at Hawthorn and just as dangerous when resting in a forward pocket. Some of his stats were truly amazing.

John Platten: a real dynamo around the packs.

Hawthorn's Dermott Brereton has the rare ability to be able to turn a game in ten minutes. He's a big-time footballer, tough and aggressive.

Many are taller than Dermott, but he competes successfully against them, playing the game as it should be played. He has plenty of fire and is very inspiring. Hawthorn recognised his leadership abilities this year by making him deputy captain. Rightly or wrongly, he tends to be the most watched footballer in the game. Perhaps he has mellowed a bit. Certainly he's got smarter. He doesn't blatantly retaliate as he sometimes used to do.

Carlton's Steve Silvagni is also in my Top 10, just edging out Collingwood's Peter Daicos, Hawthorn's John Platten and Essendon's Simon Madden. Steve is probably as good a footballer as I've ever played on. He's very desperate, has great courage, can run, jump and kick with both feet.

Contesting with Steve Silvagni. He's probably as good a footballer as I've ever played on.

Essendon's Simon Madden: among the best players of my time.

I've had some good tussles with him. I kicked ten against him the day we beat Carlton by four points at Moorabbin in 1989. It was one of the best wins I've ever been involved in. But he got even a year later. He's a natural.

## TEN BEST PLAYERS OF MY TIME

1. Greg Williams (Carlton)
2. Leigh Matthews (Hawthorn)
3. Bruce Doull (Carlton)
4. Terry Daniher (Essendon)
5. Trevor Barker (St Kilda)
6. Dale Weightman (Richmond)
7. Dermott Brereton (Hawthorn)
8. Robert Harvey (St Kilda)
9. Steve Silvagni (Carlton)
10. Danny Frawley (St Kilda)

# 32 SO YOU WANT TO PLAY
## AT FULL FORWARD

In any game I play, I try not to worry about my opponent. I know what I have to do. I try to pick out their weaknesses and use that information to my advantage.

A few backmen will try and niggle. I'm sure that's what they're all told to do. If they want to do that, that's up to them. I'm the forward and reckon the backman is there to keep an eye on me—not for me to worry about him. Obviously I'll try and chase them out and do the little team things that everyone has to do, but I never stop trying to attack.

Even if I'm getting beaten or I'm not going too well, I always try to make the play and be the aggressor. It's no good standing back and waiting for things to happen. You make your own luck and if you're willing to try a few different things so much the better. You know they're not always going to work out, but sometimes they will.

At the end of a game, I usually know how many goals and behinds I've kicked. Every full forward does—that goes with playing the position.

The same basics apply to playing at full forward as anywhere else. Rule number one is to get yourself in front whenever possible. Full forwards must contest every issue.

Obviously there will be times when you get caught behind. That happens to everyone. In cases like that, follow the basics. Punch the ball. All your team-mates become programmed and know if they see you caught behind, that the ball is going to be punched to the front of the pack. They can then time their runs accordingly.

Full forwards must always be a target for team-mates further afield. Simplicity is the key. By running into the right spaces, it gives team-mates time to deliver the ball accurately, in the right manner, without them having to turn doughnuts to do it. You've got to make it as easy for them as possible. If you can do that well, generally they will pass the ball spot-on.

Never forget that as a full forward, you're nothing without the players further afield. That's why I always scoff at suggestions that 'Lockett is a One Man Team'. It just isn't right.

Sometimes opposing coaches try to throw you off your game with unusual tactics, like those Essendon adopted at Moorabbin in 1991, when Kevin Sheedy played eight defenders and only four forwards against us. The two extras were stationed just ahead of me. It threw us right off key that day. They got a big jump on us and we never recovered.

Using a similar tactic at a ground like Waverley would be pretty impossible to achieve, but it certainly shocked us, and after kicking 34 goals in my previous three games, I was held to just four.

---

'IF RUGBY LEAGUE'S 'KING' WALLY LEWIS IS THE "EMPEROR OF LANG PARK" THEN ST KILDA'S SUPERSTAR VFL FULL FORWARD "LORD" TONY LOCKETT IS THE UNDISPUTED "MAYOR OF MOORABBIN".'

TERRY WILSON (GOLD COAST BULLETIN, 1989)

---

# 33 THE SECRETS OF SUCCESS

I suppose I kick straighter than most for goal, but it doesn't always happen that way. Just ask the boys at training. Every now and again, at the end of a night, Kenny Sheldon will get the senior 22 together and say: 'Righto, if there's any more than four misses, you've got a 400 to do', meaning an extra sprint around the ground, from goalpost to goalpost.

Most of the guys count on my shot going through, but I've missed as many as anyone! Stewie Loewe used to too, but he's straightened his kicking up now, with the help of Peter Hudson.

'Huddo' has been really good to me, too. He doesn't stick his nose in and he won't tell me anything unless he absolutely thinks it will help. He lets me do my own thing but if I go up to him and ask him for advice he's just great. He'll stand there for an hour giving tips and advice. It doesn't matter what time of night it is. He'll go out and do a bit of kicking with you long after everyone else has gone home.

Early last year, before I returned after my back injury, I trained at the club at nine o'clock every morning for a couple of weeks. Huddo was out there with me, whether it was raining or the sun was shining, kicking to me for a good hour. Nothing was too much trouble for him. He's got a really good heart. He's been really good for the club as he's a real go-getter. If something needs doing, he will go and do it. He gets the job done.

A couple of times early in that 1991 season I was missing easy shots I should have got. Huddo and I worked on a few things and my kicking straightened overnight.

I haven't got a magic method when kicking for goal, other than following the same routine each time. I find when I'm on

136

Goalkicking: it's all in your routine!

Left: Peter Hudson (left) with Kenny Sheldon. Both have been terrific. 'Huddo' will stand there for an hour giving tips and advice.

Right: Headache time: missing shots I should have got.

a roll, the ball automatically flies straight,* but I still have to be careful to go through my routine and do everything like clockwork.

One of the 'musts' when taking a set shot is to make sure you know where the mark is. Invariably the full backs on the mark will run back a little bit, before rushing at me, trying to break my concentration. Sometimes I've come in a little bit too far and all of a sudden I've sensed them running in at me. That's when you tend to falter in your run-up and stab at the ball, rather than kicking through it.

On set shots, I always go back about the same distance. You get to know within a half a metre or so where you should stand. It becomes instinctive.

When I turn around to kick for goal I always make sure to 'feel' the wind and try to gauge what it is going to do. If it is blowing pretty hard, I try to hold on for a few seconds to help me judge if it's a steady breeze or one which is fluctuating.

If there's a drop in the wind, I head straight off and kick for the goal, following all the basics, keeping my head firmly over the ball and walking in directly at the goal umpire. I figure

* In 1985, he kicked 25 goals from 26 shots.

138

When I'm on a roll, the ball automatically flies straight . . .

Sharing the ball ahead of North Melbourne's Jeff Chandler, Moorabbin, 1989.

the goal umpire is the best one to aim at as he always stands in the centre of the goals, no matter the angle. I imagine I'm kicking the ball straight at and over him.

When I get within five yards of where I'm going to kick, I'm conscious of a tuft of grass where my left foot is going to stand while I kick the ball. I always make sure it's a nice flat piece of ground and that it's directly in line with me and the umpire.

Focusing full concentration on the ball, I go for it, working to keep my body well over the ball, especially when kicking into the wind.

If I'm too far out and there is no one to pass it to, I'll have a whack at the torpedo. Otherwise, I kick drop punts almost exclusively. It's something I've always done and I find it more of a 'percentage' kick than the torp. However, the torp does fly further and when you really get on to one, you feel like you've hardly touched it. If we're allowed to have a kick before training, we invariably practise them. A lot of times, though, it's not possible, as Kenny likes us to go out together.

140

When the opportunity is there we all love to try and bomb them through, but nobody has ever kicked them like one of my first St Kilda team-mates, Glenn Brown. He was only a medium-size bloke, but could he kick a ball. He'd have no trouble regularly roosting his torpedoes 65-70 metres. I've never seen anything quite like it.

I kicked a long one in a State game against South Australia here in 1989, but I had no other option. The three-quarter time siren had gone and being 55-60 metres out on a heavy day, no other kick would have made it.

---

'JUST HOW GOOD IS TONY LOCKETT? WE WERE ALL ASKING THAT QUESTION AFTER HIS LATEST FABULOUS PERFORMANCE (10.7 AGAINST CARLTON). HIS COACH DARREL BALDOCK SAYS LOCKETT IS THE BEST HE'S SEEN AND WHO CAN ARGUE WITH THAT.'

GEOFF POULTER (*THE HERALD*, 1989)

---

# 34 CRYSTAL BALL
TIME

I've enjoyed myself at St Kilda and hopefully in the next few years we'll be able to achieve a premiership. If we can and I'm a part of it, it'll be the crowning point of my career.

This is my tenth season. If I can play another five, there's not going to be too many blokes who have played fifteen years of League football. Hopefully I can play until I'm thirty and achieve something like 200 games-plus, if things work out to plan. However, I'd want to stop before my game started to slip. Too many footballers go on too long and that's something I don't intend doing. I want to go out on a high note.

If I can play 230 or 240 games, I couldn't stop there. I'd have to keep on going to make 250. The closer I got to a target such as that, the more I'd want it. Right from the time I started, I said I'd be rapt if I could get to 250. It remains one of my key goals. After all my injuries and missed matches, realistically I may have to look at only 200 games. But you just never know— as long as the wheels stay on.

At the start of the 1992 season, I approached 150 games, so if everything falls into place in three years' time, I'll have 200 up.

To do it, I need to improve my average. In four seasons from 1988–91, after winning the 1987 Brownlow, I played only 48 of a possible 89 matches. At one stage I was twelve games ahead of 'Spud' Frawley. Now he's at least twenty matches in front of me. Until 1992, he'd hardly ever missed a game.

My fantasy is to finish football as successfully as possible. I'd like to be able to say that I've worked hard for fifteen years and done as much as I could. I want to be in a position to be able to enjoy the rest of my life. I'd like to think that I've done the right thing with my money and be in a position to cruise a little and relax. Isn't that what everyone wants to do?

Being sidelined for so many games has been a major disappointment. Watching from the grandstand is not my cup of tea, especially if we lose. But the highs mainly outweigh the lows and I wouldn't change too much about my first ten years in football. Seeing the team finish last in each of my first four years was hardly a dream start.

But you never know, our time might be happening now. I hope I can hang around and be part of it. Afterwards, I just don't know. Maybe I'll coach one day. But it'd be at kids' level first, to see if I liked it. Perhaps then I'd do it at a more senior level.

---

'ST KILDA FULL FORWARD TONY LOCKETT HAS BECOME THE SAINTS' RECESSION BUSTER. ALONG WITH NICKY WINMAR, THE SAINTS ESTIMATE LOCKETT IS WORTH AN EXTRA 6000 PEOPLE THROUGH THE TURNSTILES EACH WEEK.'

DARYL TIMMS (*HERALD-SUN*, 1991)

---

When I finish playing with St Kilda I can't see myself ever putting the boots on again, even in Ballarat. Once I finish here, that'll be it. I'd only be letting myself down and it would be difficult to meet people's expectations to go on elsewhere.

Whatever happens, I'll continue to be myself. I reckon it's no good trying to kid yourself and be someone that you're not. A few things haven't worked out for me, but there's not much I regret. Not everyone runs true to perfect.

---

'IF THERE'S A FOOTBALL HEAVEN, 25,000 ST KILDA FANS WERE IN IT YESTERDAY. THEIR IDOL, TONY LOCKETT, WAS BACK—AND FIRING.'

KEN PIESSE, AFTER LOCKETT'S 12-GOAL COMEBACK AGAINST THE ADELAIDE CROWS (*SUNDAY HERALD-SUN*, 1991)

---

# 35 EIGHT DAYS A WEEK

Time-tables and I don't always get on. But I do my best to meet my commitments. I'm not a great one for keeping a diary, but I always have a list of what's on that day on the door of the fridge.

My manager, Robert Hession, is in touch virtually daily with things that are coming up. Here's an example of my day-to-day routine, taken the week leading up to our first game—and first win—of the 1992 season, against Essendon at Waverley.

**SUNDAY, 15 MARCH**

Our last practice match before the actual season start. We play Carlton in Burnie. I kick only one goal before coming off at half-time. My fitness isn't a problem. I feel good and have a good warm-up before the game. But I don't want to do too much, as I'd played only twice previously, including the Sunday before when I had just a half against the Brisbane Bears.

I'd done better in that first game, kicking five goals. It was just an average performance, though. I was happy to take a few marks and kick a few goals. Richard Champion played at full back. He's got pace and is very aggressive. He didn't hold my jumper, either. He's one of the few who don't. He's a good, honest goer.

For the Carlton game, the wind is blowing straight down the ground. Some of the gusts must be more than 100 m.p.h. We are narrowly beaten but it isn't any big deal. I don't take much notice of practice match form. A lot of players are still finding their feet and trying to find a bit of touch. We'd deliberately played a couple of matches in a row on a Sunday as our first three games in the proper season are Sunday games.

144

The ball hardly ventures up my end in the second quarter and I was off after that. I'm still not 100 per cent fit. I'm aiming to reach my peak fitness by rounds six and seven so I can continue to hold my form throughout the season rather than peaking too early.

MONDAY

A 6 a.m. rise and into all the normal duties around the property with my friend, Darren McDonald. Two of the injured dogs, Bluey and Jack, need a bit of machining. Ten minutes on each sore spot. We want to trial Jack later in the week to see how he's progressing.

Have a swim at the Cranbourne pool. Forty laps—a good kilometre's worth. It takes half hour to 40 minutes. I don't do them straight out, just 10 at a time with a minute's pause in between. Rest for the remainder of the day before looking after the dogs again later on.

TUESDAY

Attend a promotion for Puma with sporting identities who have come from all round Australia for the launch of the new Puma Disc System, a twenty-first century set of runners guaranteed to put an extra spring in your step. They are super runners, too.

Do a TV interview with Michael Roberts and Channel Seven about Sunday's first game, before going down to see Stan Nicholes for my normal weights work-out. His place is in Caulfield and pretty handy to everything. He puts me through a three-quarter hour work-out. It's a fairly punishing session, but one I'm almost starting to enjoy.

I go there every night before training. Stan has been a big help. I hope that over the next four or five months, his extra work will really show. He has trained some great athletes over the years. He used to be our weights adviser at the footy club. Now his son, Peter, does that.

I'm working mainly on my upper body strength. I'm getting a little bit older now and want to make sure I maintain my strength for marking duels.

Off to training, where we do a lot of limbering up and skills work. You can feel the extra sense of excitement. Pre-season training is over. From Sunday, it's the real thing.

WEDNESDAY

Channel Seven organises a goalkicking duel at Glenferrie Oval, to be shown on the following Sunday's 'Sportsworld' show. I compete with Jason Dunstall, Bill Brownless and Peter Daicos. Allen Jakovich pulls out because of an injured back.

I hadn't kicked that many for goal at training and there's

145

quite a headwind blowing. Jason Dunstall was kicking on his home ground and had the inside knowledge so I'm very happy to win. Everyone's in good spirits and nice and relaxed. They are all good blokes. It's totally different from when we're on the field.

We are paid $500 each in appearance money with $2000 going to the winner. I get there for first with a big torpedo which goes straight through, post-high. I'm pretty happy with that one.

Train that night at Waverley. Usually, the Tuesday or Wednesday—depending on when we play—is our hardest night, but it's a little lighter today, with our first game just four days away. Playing at Waverley, as well, you really need to be as fresh as possible in the legs.

We do a lot of running the ball up and down the ground and generally getting the feel of the surface. I know I'm short of the fitness level I'd like to be at, but I'm getting better and better with each training session.

THURSDAY

A quiet sort of day. Up at six to look after the dogs. I do another swimming session in the pool. Just 25 laps this time. Get out the mower for an hour and get the place looking neat again.

FRIDAY

Go to Warragul with a mate of mine, Kevin Kelly, to trial Jack (or Wild Scene) and one of his dogs, as well. Jack has had a bad injury and it's taking a lot of time to come right. He's a tough sort of dog but he still pulls up lame. We have to have another plan of attack and see if we can fix it.

Warragul is a big safe track. It's not like some trial tracks which are a bit run-down. At Cranbourne, there's usually a heap of people there and you have to sit and wait. The dogs get very excited and carried away with themselves. Jack is a very quick dog and needs a bit of room to gallop. We're first there, do the job and come home again.

In the afternoon, I do another session with Stan before going off to training by quarter to five. Twenty-two black guernseys are handed out. We know that the twenty who are going to be named come from this 22. The rest of the boys get red jumpers. They are going to play in the reserves. A few are disappointed not to be handed the black ones, but that's only human nature.

The senior group go out on the track first and train for about forty minutes before coming in to do a quick session of weights, and the other group takes the track. Ken Sheldon tells everyone where they are playing and who the unlucky two are. We don't have a team dinner or anything like that. Ken just wants us to rest and be ready for action on Sunday.

146

A very relaxed day at home. Building up the energy reserves. Vicki comes down from Ballarat in the afternoon and prepares a big bowl of pasta for Saturday night. I usually have some sort of spaghetti dish the night before the game.

We watch a good movie that night, Kenny Rogers in *The Gambler*. It starts at 8.30 and I thought it was going to finish at 10.30 but it goes for three-and-a-half hours. I record the last hour and a bit.

SUNDAY

Up earlier than usual for a match day. Darren takes care of the dogs. He always does on match days. The nerves have started to get to me a little bit, probably because it's the first game. I didn't sleep too well. We watch the rest of the movie before going out to Waverley for the footy.

It looks like being a lovely day. The sun is out. There isn't too much wind about, either. Arrive well in time for the 12.30 p.m. team meeting. Pre-match, I'm very confident that we can win, even though Essendon has had the wood on us for as long as I've been playing.

---

'TONY IS PLACED UNDER TREMENDOUS PHYSICAL PRESSURE EVERY WEEK FOR NO REWARD. I'D LIKE TO SPEAK TO BILL [DELLER] AND CLEAR UP THE SITUATION. NO-ONE CAN KEEP THEIR COOL FOR LONG UNDER THAT SORT OF PRESSURE.'

ST KILDA COACH DARREL BALDOCK, AFTER THE MATCH AGAINST CARLTON, 1988

---

With all due respect to Essendon's great champions such as Simon Madden and Terry Daniher (who we also thought would be playing), I feel our younger players will have more run in their legs.

Waverley Park can be a good ground, but it can be terrible, too, especially if the wind is blowing and it's wet. In cases like that, it's a big open hole. It's not much fun at all.

Today, the conditions are good, although the ground is as hard as I've ever struck it. Usually they leave a nice covering of grass, but not today. (I finished up with gashed knees and a cut down my leg, but nothing really serious.) It's also pretty hot for footy, about 30 degrees.

We're nice and keyed up beforehand. I don't shake hands with my opponent Brad Fox. If he'd offered his hand, I would have. But he didn't. I shake hands with some blokes. It just depends what sort of mood I'm in.

147

There'd been publicity pre-match on how close Fox was going to play me. It was soon obvious he was under strict instructions. There were quite a few times during the game where I would have loved to have given it to this bloke, but I have to keep my head. I'm no value to myself or the club sitting on the sidelines with a four-week suspension against me. It's very hard to do at the time, but I am old enough and mature enough now to turn a blind eye.

I'm still not going to be intimidated by them, though. Whatever they give me, I'll give them just as much back. This bloke gave me the impression that he didn't want to do any rough stuff—that he was just doing it under sufferance.

We had a few wrestles but that was about it. The umpires could call it unduly rough play, but you'd be pretty stiff to go on that. I was just showing my physical strength. If he wanted to party, I was prepared to accommodate him.

Overall, I guess he performed quite well, but I still kicked seven and I was quite happy to get out of the game with what I'd done. If you can kick seven every week you're pretty well laughing.

They don't play eight defenders this time—as at Moorabbin in 1991—but both ruckmen, Salmon and Madden, drop back regularly. Sheedy thinks he's pretty smart the way he does things. Many times, though, it backfires, I reckon.

Even when they get to three goals ahead, I'm confident we have the fitness behind us to win the game, especially playing at Waverley where we can exploit them a little bit more.

We win after a pretty even game and are very satisfied later. We had lots of good players. It was a real team effort, though guys like Nicky Winmar, Micky Dwyer and Rob Harvey all do very well. So did Stewie Loewe. Up till half-time, we'd only got the ball out of the middle four or five times out of 19. If we had done better there, we would have won more easily. There are parts of our game we need to change around and really work on.

It's good coming out of the game with a win, knowing that there's a lot more improvement in us yet. I'd run out of legs just after half-time. I know I have a lot of improving to do. But it's no good me peaking right at the start of the season.

The main thing is that we won the game. I'd rather only kick a few and win the game, rather than kick a bag and lose it. It all gets down to winning and losing the game. As long as you have contributed, that's all you can do.

Afterwards, the guys, their wives and girlfriends go back briefly to the Village Green for a drink, followed by our jumper presentation back at the club. Peter Hudson gives out numbers

148

one to ten, Ken Sheldon, eleven to twenty and Danny Frawley the others. It's mainly an in-house, low-key thing—not as big as it's been in previous years.

Ken talks about how we need to set up our position in the first half of the year. Our immediate target, after the first three games, is to be no worse than two-one. After Footscray at the Western Oval we have the West Coast Eagles, which is going to be a very hard game, as is Hawthorn at Moorabbin. But if we can get on top of them early, the sky is the limit.

We win after a pretty even game. Walking off with Nicky Winmar (obscured) and first-gamer Stevie Clark.

149

# 36 VICKI AND I

I've been with Vicki now for eight years. She was only sixteen or seventeen when we met. She's always been good. She's a quiet type and puts up with a lot. I don't think I'd have achieved what I have today without her.

Vicki and I.

A few times I've gone off the tracks and she's always been there to restore control.

She comes from Ballarat, too. I met her one day at a hairdressing salon, where she was working. She was a friend of a friend. A whole group of us went to the beach together at Christmas, 1984. She was there, too. It just went from there.

She didn't take too much notice of the footy at the time. Now she's one of my staunchest fans, along with my Mum and Dad and family. She manages a hairdressing salon in Ballarat and plays a lot of sport herself.

# PLUGGERISMS

Bad press:   When guys in the media have a go at me, generally over my weight. These gents haven't always played the game . . .

Bandwagon:   What the supporters jump on—and off—depending on how their team is going.

Beef:   Not seeing eye-to-eye with someone else.

Biff:   Punch.

Blue:   Confrontation, argument, heated incident, donnybrook. *See* Scrag.

Brick wall:   Almost impossible to pass. Opposition players who kick in the direction of guys like David Grant and Danny Frawley know what I mean.

Built like a proverbial you-know-what:   Huge.

Come the dirty:   Bite, gouge, claw, kick, king hit, throw a haymaker at.

Cooling my heels:   Sidelined.

Did my cruet:   Blew up.

Earned his stripes:   Win respect.

Giant hiccup:   Losing a few games on end; not kicking straight for any period of time.

Go down like a sack of spuds:   Collapse, as if shot.

Heat:   Pressure.

Laying down: Taking a dive, often to win a free kick; sometimes to avoid any involvement in a blue.

Pinged: Reported.

Savage: Angry.

Scrag: Niggle, wrestle.

Short wick: Tending to see red, without counting to ten!

Sodas: Easy shots at goal.

Spot-on player: Gun footballer.

Thrown to the wolves: Playing or coaching at a level beyond one's immediate capabilities.

Turning doughnuts: Running around in circles, doubling back, mucking around with the ball.

Twig: Realise.

Whack (at a torpedo): Let one go.

Wooden spoon contention: Too close to the bottom for comfort; somewhere where we don't want to be.

# TONY LOCKETT'S
# GOALKICKING RECORD

| ROUND | 1983 | 1984 | 1985 | 1986 | 1987 | 1988 | 1989 | 1990 | 1991 |
|---|---|---|---|---|---|---|---|---|---|
| 1 | — | 7 | 2 | 1 | 2 | 4 | 9 | 10 | INJ |
| 2 | — | 3 | 0 | SUS | 5 | SUS | 10 | 9 | INJ |
| 3 | — | 6 | 3 | SUS | 3 | SUS | 8 | 2 | INJ |
| 4 | 2 | 4 | 4 | 7 | 12 | SUS | 5 | 7 | INJ |
| 5 | 1 | 7 | 2 | 6 | 5 | 5 | 5 | 7 | BYE |
| 6 | — | 2 | SUS | 5 | 0 | 3 | 6 | 5 | INJ |
| 7 | — | 7 | 5 | 2 | 6 | 0 | 6 | 7 | 12 |
| 8 | — | 0 | 0 | 0 | 7 | 7 | 9 | 5 | 10 |
| 9 | — | INJ | 3 | INJ | 2 | 7 | 12 | INJ | 12 |
| 10 | — | 6 | 7 | INJ | 5 | 9 | SUS | INJ | 4 |
| 11 | — | 3 | 6 | 3 | 9 | 0 | SUS | INJ | 7 |
| 12 | 0 | 2 | 7 | 0 | 3 | INJ | SUS | INJ | 5 |
| 13 | 2 | 7 | 6 | 4 | 3 | INJ | SUS | INJ | 8 |
| 14 | 2 | INJ | 3 | 4 | 1 | INJ | 3 | INJ | 5 |
| 15 | 3 | 3 | 6 | 1 | 5 | INJ | 5 | INJ | 8 |
| 16 | 0 | 3 | 5 | 4 | 8 | INJ | INJ | INJ | 5 |
| 17 | INJ | 2 | 6 | 4 | 9 | INJ | INJ | 3 | 2 |
| 18 | 1 | 2 | 1 | 8 | 8 | INJ | INJ | 3 | 5 |
| 19 | 0 | 2 | 3 | 1 | 8 | INJ | INJ | 4 | 1 |
| 20 | 5 | 4 | 1 | 1 | 3 | INJ | INJ | 3 | BYE |
| 21 | 2 | 3 | 5 | 4 | 8 | INJ | INJ | INJ | 13 |
| 22 | 1 | 4 | 4 | 5 | 5 | INJ | INJ | INJ | 10 |
| 23 | | | | | | | | | FLU |
| 24 | | | | | | | | | 11 |
| SEF | | | | | | | | | 9 |
| | | | | | | | | | |
| GOALS | 19 | 77 | 79 | 60 | 117 | 35 | 78 | 65 | 127 |
| MATCHES | 12 | 20 | 21 | 18 | 22 | 8 | 11 | 12 | 17 |

TOTAL GAMES = 141 (1983–91)
TOTAL GOALS = 657.

154

# TONY LOCKETT:

## POTTED CAREER HIGHLIGHTS

**1966:** Born 9 March, Ballarat.

**1973:** Debuts aged seven, for North Ballarat under-12s.

**1976:** Plays for St Kilda's Little League team for the first time.

**1978:** Plays his one-hundredth junior game.

**1981:** Aged fifteen, kicks six goals in his first open-age match for North Ballarat reserves.

**1982:** Named 'champion junior footballer' at St Kilda's junior development carnival. Lifted into the North Ballarat A-grade side, aged 16, he kicks 3.3 from a forward pocket against Golden Point—including a goal from his first kick in senior football, at the 11-minute mark of the opening term. Also kicks six goals in a half against Maddingley-Bacchus Marsh before dislocating two fingers and leaving the ground at half-time.

**1983:** On arrival at Moorabbin, boots seven goals on debut with St Kilda reserves against North Melbourne. Is named in the senior team against Geelong. Kicks two goals on debut, including a goal with his first kick in League football. Plays in a forward pocket beside Mark Jackson.

**1984:** Kicks 7.4 in the opening game against Essendon, the best season start by a St Kilda player, surpassing the previous best of six goals held by eight players, including legends Darrel Baldock and Bill Mohr. Is named (after 26 VFL games) as a replacement for the injured Paul Salmon in Victoria's squad to play Western Australia, but misses final selection.

**1985:** Kicks six goals from six kicks against Carlton's Steve Silvagni. Plays for Victoria for the first time, kicking one goal

155

Contesting with Danny Hughes in the 1989 State game in Melbourne.

Winning the VFL Players' Association's Most Valuable Player Medal, 1987.

against WA in Perth. Kicks six goals representing the Premier's All-Stars in a game against the All-Australian Aboriginals, under lights at the MCG.

**1986:** Boots five goals in a quarter against North Melbourne (in 18 minutes of the second term). Finishes with eight for the day.

**1987:** Is appointed deputy vice-captain to Danny Frawley. Amasses 117 goals for the season, including 12.3 against Melbourne, a new St Kilda club record. Wins the John Coleman medal. After kicking nine goals against Essendon, Bomber coach Kevin Sheedy says he's the best full forward since Doug Wade. Is one of Victoria's best players against South Australia in Adelaide, being moved into the ruck in the last quarter with immediate result. Becomes the first full forward to win the Brownlow Medal. Ron Barassi says: 'Tony Lockett has the potential to be one of the greatest full forwards of all time'. Also wins St Kilda's best and fairest. Coach Darrel Baldock says: 'Tony was a focal point in every attack we made and regardless of how the ball was delivered to him, he would convert it virtually every time'. Signs three-year contract.

**1988:** Named club vice-captain, suspension and injury shorten his season to just eight games, his least successful year on record.

**1989:** Kicks seventy goals in the opening nine rounds, including twelve against the Eagles. Is third best and fairest. Kicks five goals for Victoria against S.A. in front of more than 90,000 fans at the MCG.

**1990:** Signs a new five-year contract, virtually ensuring that he'll play out his whole career at St Kilda. Suffers whiplash in a car accident near Smeaton, 28 km north of Ballarat after returning from Bendigo where he'd been trialling several of his greyhounds.

**1991:** Kicks 12.6 against Adelaide Crows in his first match of the season, including nine to half time. Amasses twelve, ten and twelve goals in his first three games of the season (rounds seven, eight and nine), equalling the feats of Bob Pratt and John Coleman, who also had kicked three ten-or-more tallies in consecutive weeks. Boots 100 goals for the second time in his career, including a career-best 13.3 against Carlton in his fifteenth match of the year. Only South Melbourne's Bob Pratt had kicked one hundred in quicker time (thirteen matches in 1934). Wins the Coleman medal, with 127 goals, a personal-best effort. Kicks nine goals v. Geelong in the elimination final, the most by a St Kilda player in a final. Wins best and fairest for the second time and heads St Kilda's goalkicking for a seventh year. His effort of passing 10 or more goals six times for the season is also a 'first'. Wins All-Australian selection.

**1992:** Named vice-captain, he kicks another double-figure tally against the Crows, five of his 10 goals coming in the third quarter. Is acquitted of a striking charge on Carlton's Matthew Hogg. Is named in State team to play WA after earlier announcing his unavailability to Ted Whitten, the Victorian selection chairman.

Top: A one-hander against North Melbourne in a trial match, March 1990.

Bottom: Waverley, 1990. David Rhys-Jones just happened to be in the wrong place at the wrong time. Sorry Rhys.

# DISTINCTIONS

- Brownlow Medal 1987;
- John Coleman Medallist 1987 (117 goals) and 1991 (127);
- St Kilda best and fairest 1987 and 1991;
- All-Australian 1991;
- St Kilda's leading goalkicker seven times.

## MATCH RECORD

|  | GAMES | GOALS | AVERAGE |
|---|---|---|---|
| DAY MATCHES | 141 | 657 | 4.65 |
| NIGHT MATCHES | 6 | 17 | 2.83 |
| STATE GAMES | 3 | 7 | 2.33 |

## SEASON-BY-SEASON

| SEASON | GAMES | GOALS | BEHINDS | GAME AVERAGE |
|---|---|---|---|---|
| 1983 | 12 | 19 | 15 | 1.58 goals |
| 1984 | 20 | 77 | 44 | 3.85 |
| 1985 | 21 | 79 | 22 | 3.76 |
| 1986 | 18 | 60 | 29 | 3.3 |
| 1987 | 22 | 117 | 52 | 5.31 |
| 1988 | 8 | 35 | 19 | 4.37 |
| 1989 | 11 | 78 | 24 | 7.09 |
| 1990 | 12 | 65 | 34 | 5.41 |
| 1991 | 17 | 127 | 51 | 7.47 |
| TOTALS | 141 | 657 | 290 | 4.65 |

## SUSPENSIONS

| 1985 | Striking Laurie Serafini (Fitzroy) | One week |
| 1986 | Striking Rick Kennedy (Footscray) | Two weeks |
| 1988 | Striking Grant Lawrie (Fitzroy) | Three weeks |
| 1989 | Striking Guy McKenna (West Coast) | Four weeks |

# A DECADE OF SAINTS

## (My teammates, 1983-92)

ABLETT, Geoff
ALLEN, Tim
AMOORE, Geoff
ANTROBUS, Tony
ARNOL, Jody

BARKER, Trevor
BENNETT, Andrew
BENNETT, John
BLEES, Michael
BOLAND, Glenn
BOWEY, Brett
BROWN, Glenn
BROWN, Peter
BUCKLEY, Mark
BURKE, Nathan
BURNS, Greg

CAHIR, Gerard
CARBONE, Frank
CHIRON, Dean
CLARK, Stephen
COLLINS, Jonathan
COGHLAN, Frank
COWIE, Darrell
CRAVEN, Danny
CREBBIN, Tom
CRONAN, Phil
CROSS, Andrew
CROW, Max
CUMMINGS, Steven
CUNNINGHAM, Geoff
CUNNINGHAM, Daryl
CURTAIN, Peter

DANIELS, Jayson
DARGIE, Ian
DAVIES, Darren
DEVONPORT, Craig
DI PETTA, Aldo
DONALD, Luke
DOYLE, Greg
DUNNE, Jeff
DWYER, Mark
DWYER, "Mick"

ELPHINSTONE, Robert
EVANS, Anthony

FAVIER, John
FIDLER, Geoff
FLETCHER, Adrian
FLANIGAN, Darren
FODE, Gordon
FORD, Alister
FORD, Michael
FOSCHINI, Silvio
FOYSTER, Mark
FRAWLEY, Danny
FREEMAN, Peter

GAMBLE, Mark
GARRETT, Chris
GELLIE, Graeme
GEORGIOU, John
GLADMAN, Rodney
GOTCH, Brad
GRANT, David
GREEN, Warwick
GREIG, Dean

HANDLEY, Robert
HARDING, Paul
HARRIS, Bernie
HARVEY, Robert
HILTON, Jeff

INGLETON, Ben

JACKSON, Mark
JEFFREY, Russell
JENKIN, Alan
JOBLING, Andrew
JONES, Bob
JONES, Greg
JONES, Warren

KEEBLE, Robert
KICKETT, Dale
KIEL, Peter
KINK, Rene
KITSCHKE, Damien
KOURKOUMELIS, Spiro
KRAKOUER, Jim

LAMB, Jamie
LANE, Greg

161

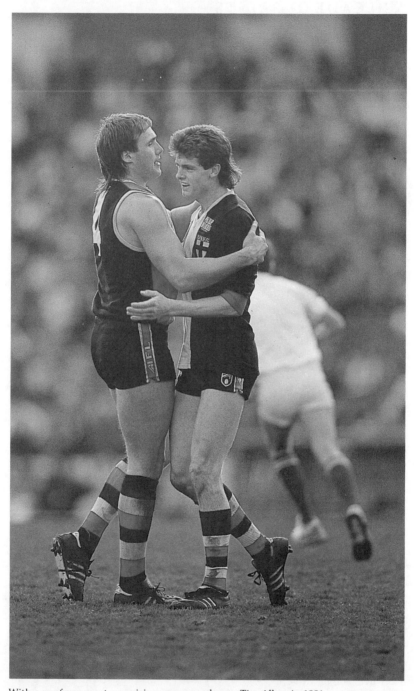

With one of our most promising younger players Tim Allen, in 1991.

LAWRIE, Grant
LISTER, Christian
LITTLER, Brendan
LOEWE, Stewart

McADAM, Gilbert
McADAM, Greg
McASEY, Chris
McCONVILLE, Peter
McNICHOLL, Dermott
MACE, Robert
MacILWAIN, Geoff
MacMILLAN, Glenn
MANNING, Andrew
MARCOU, Alex
MEEHAN, Simon
MELESSO, Peter
MIDDLEMISS, Glen
MISSO, Enrico
MORRIS, Russell
MORWOOD, Paul
MUIR, Robert
MULLER, Ian

NARKLE, Phil
NEAL, Robert
NEWPORT, Stephen
NIXON, Ricky

O'DONNELL, Simon
ODGERS, Gary
OWEN, Rod

PACKHAM, Greg
PAGE, Paul
PECKETT, Jason

PEKIN, Tim
PETER-BUDGE, John
PIRRIE, Stephen

QUIRK, Michael

RALPHSMITH, Sean
RICE, Dean
RIGGS, Jon
ROBERTS, Michael
RUSSO, Peter

SARAU, Jeff
SCHULTZ, John
SEXTON, Damian
SHANAHAN, Jamie
SHARP, Greg
SHELDON, Ken
SIDEBOTTOM, Allan
SIMPSON, Sean
SMITH, Rohan
SMITH, Terry

TAYLOR, Kain
TEMAY, Paul
TILLEY, Paul
TURNER, Steve

VIDOVIC, Lazar

WILSON, Brian
WINBANKS, David
WINMAR, Nicky
WINTON, Brian
WITTEY, David

# GO PLUGGER, GO

(Sung to tune of 'Johnny B Goode')

1.
Way down at old Moorabbin there's a great spearhead
He's the one that's always worn the black, white and red
Now some may say he looks a little overfed
But he can bag a sausage roll while standing on his head.
Now some full-forwards lead into the pocket all day
But they can't play the way that Tony Lockett can play.

Chorus:
Go, go—go Plugger, go, go, go
—Plugger be good.

2.
He used to practise with a chewed-up plastic football
He used to kick it thru the window from the time he was small
His mamma used to feed him on cream buns and steak
Sayin' this'll build you up for all the marks you will take.
He never ever learned to weave and baulk so good
But he could kick a bag of goals like he was choppin' wood.

Chorus.

(Courtesy Greg Champion and
The Coodabeen Champions).